Inspire;

reflective essays by students that learn differently

Foreword by Jena Young

RiSE Scholarship Foundation, Inc.

D1449275

DEDICATION

To the many students who have second-guessed their potential.

CHALLENGES ARE OFTEN LIKE CLIMBING A
MOUNTAIN.

YOU CLIMB AND EVERY SO OFTEN YOU SLIP
BACK A LITTLE. BUT IF YOU KEEP ON
CLIMBING, YOU WILL GET TO THE TOP OF THAT
MOUNTAIN.

Quotes and Essays By High School Students that Learn Differently.

FOREWORD

This book was an idea that my husband and I discussed at length 6 years ago. At that time one of our children was struggling in elementary school both with the subject matter of the class, primarily reading and spelling, but also with the teachers. As an infant he had been terribly ill with an immune deficiency that caused countless infections and affected not only his attendance at school, but also his hearing, speech and overall health. After years of monitoring his health and finally finding some amazing doctors that were able to meet his needs, we were able to send him to school regularly.

That feeling of relief was short lived as we began receiving phone calls from his teachers, notes home via book bags, and emails that he was not sitting still in his chair, not paying attention and doing poorly on his weekly spelling tests. These were just a few communications we had with the teachers and I am sure if you have picked up this book they sound all too familiar! I am not saying these were not accurate, I am just saying we were at a loss of what to do for him! My husband and I felt somewhat helpless and not sure where to turn for advice.

Our first thought was when did first grade get so tough? This experience was new to us and while maybe we had not made the best grades as students ourselves, this did not seem like the elementary school experience we remembered. To us, it seemed that we were the only ones having so much trouble. When we were called into the principal's office, we certainly had no reassurance that there were so many other families having the same feelings.

We had our son academically tested, and like so many others students with LD, he scored in the above average range to even superior range in his ability. The question was why was he not showing this at school? Why was there such a disconnect? And more importantly, how were we going to ensure that he would be successful in school?

In this anxiety-ridden environment most of us live today, this was a freighting time for us. Where could he go to school to best suit his needs? Why were they recommending Occupational Therapy and what is OT anyway? What in the world is an IEP? And so on…

All of this was overwhelming and confusing to say the least. I was at a loss. How is he going to graduate, if first grade is so hard?

Around this same time, I was in charge of organizing a large party for my garden club and was helping arrange flowers, which seemed silly because I could not get the knot out of my stomach. "Why has that teacher called me AGAIN", I thought. Frustrated, I tried to put it out of my mind and just enjoy the night with some friends. At that point, a friend asked me how the kids were and how school was going. After a deep breathe, I said that our son had recently been diagnosed with dyslexia and it was a tough year at school for him. She smiled and without even thinking twice said,

" Oh, my daughter has dyslexia and is now at college and is doing really well in school, socially and having a great time."

That quick statement may not sound earth shattering to you, but it was just what I needed! The room stopped and I could have pulled out my pen and paper right there! I was overcome with emotions! I wanted to hear more, and I wanted to hear how she did it. How did she overcome the odds?

Going home that night, I could not get it out of my mind, her daughter is thriving and of course there have to be others that are doing the same! What worked for her? Was it the school she attended? Was it finding a therapy or a modality like Orton-Gilligham that helped her through it? Was it finding a teacher that spurred her on?

As the weeks progressed I wondered, what if there were other students like her and families like my friend that would be willing to share what worked for them? What if these students could tell my son, others, and me in the same situation what their journey entailed and what was beneficial to them? It really came down to finding a way for kids, students and families to share their stories… to mentor, if you will, others that needed guidance.

Yes, I know we often hear of the success of the CEO's, movie stars, and professional athletes that have been able to thrive through their ADHD or LD, and I am not discounting their struggles in the least; however, I wanted to share the everyday and often overlooked students in our schools, our cities, our communities that have a story to tell! This intrigue and the quest for those answers lead my husband and me to create the RiSE Scholarship Foundation, Inc. in 2010.

RiSE is a non-profit organization that is a resource for students with learning differences. Our goal is to reward students who have shown determination and resiliency in dealing with their learning differences and we do this by providing scholarship reward opportunities for students in high school who are applying to 4-year Colleges or Universities in the United States. RiSE was formed to bring awareness to the success stories of so many terrific students, and to help share what has worked for them. It is to not only applaud them on their hard work and efforts, but also additionally share their success with others that can benefit.

Today, we believe that there is much more attention and focus on the fact that everyone learns differently. It makes us unique. It makes us who we are. As a headmaster recently expressed to me, "School is about the only time in our life that we have to be good at everything." It is true! Individually we all have our strengths and weaknesses and if we lean on the strengths not only will they outweigh our deficits, but also they will make us who we are meant to be! Many more teachers, parents, students and even the community as a whole know that we all can learn, we just need to think outside the box and find what makes each student be the best they can be!

At RiSE we have connected with thousands of families, schools, educators and students nationwide with the mission of helping the students with specific learning disabilities (LD) since that is our initial passion. In 2013, after continuously being contacted by equally qualified and impressive students on the Autism Spectrum, we were able to expand RiSE and add a scholarship opportunity for students that have a diagnosis of Autism Spectrum Disorder (ASD). Inside the book you will see a letter that was written to us by a parent of a child with Asperger Syndrome that added to the momentum we already had, to go forth with this branch of RiSE.

We realized that although ASD is a different diagnosis than LD, it is an area of families looking for stories of hope and encouragement. The plans for the future of RiSE are to grow in both areas offering helpful and useful information as well as an opportunity for scholarship awards for those furthering their education by pursuing a college degree.

Many times a LD, ADHD, or an Autism diagnosis is undetected, leaving children feeling less than adequate. This is not only preventable but also truly tragic. The difficulties these children face is obvious in our everyday schools. Outside of the school system these educational deficiencies, coupled with low self-esteem, add to proven higher high school dropout rates. Needlessly, many of these students ending up living in poverty and enter the prison system for reasons that could be prevented. This is a tragedy for each individual child, but also for the families and our community. With more awareness to this topic and more education for teachers and parents, these statistics can be reversed.

Our hope is that this book opens a conversation and brings mindfulness that we all are similar, we all are able to learn, and we all have something important to share! Through these students' respective notes which were meant for others in similar situations, we hope not only will you find practical suggestions, but that you will be INSPIRED!

Very Sincerely,

Jena Young

Co- Founder of RiSE Scholarship Foundation, Inc.

P.S. By the way, as I write this, our teenage son is working as a camp leader in Jackson Hole, Wyoming this summer after finishing a terrific year of school! Not only has his health dramatically improved, he is over 6 feet tall, loves to read (most anything that has to do with the outdoors), and we rarely get a call from his teacher!

HAVING A LEARNING DISABILITY HAS MADE ME MORE COMPASSIONATE, MORE AWARE OF THE CHALLENGES OTHER FACE, A BETTER PEOPLE PERSON.

INTRODUCTION

The following is a grouping of essays that were written in response to the essay questions included on the applications for the RiSE Scholarship Foundation, Inc. Award. The author's intent was to give advice to others from their personal experience with having a learning difference.

We are hopeful that you, as the reader, see their personal strength and perseverance in each of the essays. The writers, who were high school seniors when they shared these with RiSE, have not only accepted that they have been diagnosed with a learning disability or having Asperger Syndrome, but have become stronger because of these "roadblocks" as one author calls their differences. If you have a LD or not, the following notes are a glimpse into the minds of students who see the world filled with opportunity and who are eager to overcome any obstacles that stand in their way.

Some of the essays have been edited for the sake of the book formatting and to reserve the privacy of the authors.

1

To a student recently diagnosed with an learning disability to begin, I must say good luck. Any journey through your life needs it. The path that they just found themselves standing in front of is very different then the path everyone else will follow but it is no less profitable and it is not isolated. A learning difference is exactly that, a difference. It is neither good nor bad. It simply is.

I have suffered from dysgraphia for my entire life, I can't spell, I can barely write in a way that others can understand, I will think one letter and write another. Basically I shouldn't be able to pass an English class. But I have, in fact I have been on honor roll since sixth grade and am number 8 in my class. It is not impossible. It is just a bit harder than it is for everyone else. My learning difference is my dirty little secret but it is also my super power.

What you have to do is keep your head up and keep walking, find your niche, and become friends with my favorite word: COPING, and more than anything : Ask for help.

Keeping your head up is simple; You have to look ahead and realize that this is not the end of the world. You can only see what everyone else is throwing at you if you look up. The hardest part of finding out you are different is coming to terms with what that means. Sometimes it can take the longest time but in the end it will be what you are most proud of. Admit that you have a difference, whether you call it a learning difference or a disability, it is a part of you and that will not change. So don't look at it like a secret you have to keep from everyone because you think they will call you stupid. Make it your super power.

I have my own language because of mine; it follows no written dictionary but makes perfect sense. This doesn't need to be the end of the world. As silly as it seems just close your eyes, take a deep breath, then take the other path. A niche is your place in the world. It is one of the best things you can find because once you do it becomes that much harder to feel like an outsider.

Coping, I have to say that it is the most amazing word in the English dictionary, because that is exactly what we have to do. Eventually we get very good at it. I had to find a way to remember how to spell things. When I was little I would trace words out on sand paper, now I'll spell them out in sign language. It's a tactual connection. Coping is not a cover up for a learning difference it is a combination of survival techniques. We do not walk on the same path that everyone else follows and because of that the world is more in tune with those who do not have differences so we have to find a way to fit into that world without losing who we are.

If only one thing can be taken away from this I do hope it is this. Ask for help. The support from those around you is the most important thing anyone could have. Without it you can get lost and not know your way out. It doesn't matter who you ask, your teachers, your parents, your friends. All that matters is that you do. If you do not ask no one will know that you are struggling, they will not know how to help. You have to take a proactive approach to your learning. I know it's hard and embarrassing, I hate asking for help. I told that to one of my friends one day and now they ask if I need help every time they think I'm struggling. That is something that I am thankful for all the time. **Don't struggle on your own when help is only a few words away.**

The last advice I can give is to the parents of the newly diagnosed student. They cannot do it alone. Simply looking up what they were diagnosed with online can make a world of difference. Being told what you have a sociologist is not the same as hearing it from your parents. If they can come to you with questions and the problems they are having at school, it can make the greatest difference. It could be the thing that results in them succeeding beyond your wildest dreams or being so lost that they give up. I know that I would not be where I am today without the support of my mother and grandmother.

2

Children, newly diagnosed with a learning difference, need a message of hope, encouragement and acceptance. Using my personal experiences of struggles, challenges, and successes would be the basis of advice that I would want to give these children.

I would like to share with a child newly diagnosed with a learning difference that as a young child, I was diagnosed with dyslexia and that I struggled with low self-esteem for several years, as I did not feel that I was as smart as others. Many times I would become discouraged because I felt it was unfair that I had to work so hard to read and write. I was embarrassed because I had to be pulled out of my class each day to attend a "special reading class" (dyslexia program). I just wanted to be "normal."

Also, I would share that being properly diagnosed with my learning difference was the best thing that could have happened to me. Although it was awkward for me to have to go to a special class every day, I began to see the progress I was making in my reading and writing. My diagnosis allowed me to get the assistance that I needed to be successful. My dyslexia teacher helped me understand why I learned differently than others. She helped me realize that with proper instruction and use of reading strategies, I could succeed as other students.

I would want a child, recently diagnosed with a learning difference, to know that my attitude about my learning difference changed and has allowed me to be a stronger student. Knowing and accepting that I would always be dyslexic and that reading and writing would always be a challenge put me on a path to prove that I was just as capable as everyone else. This drive and determination helped me face learning challenges and allowed me to achieve great academic success – despite having a learning difference. I remain dedicated to my studies and have found areas that I excel in, despite my difference. As far as reading and writing, which is a part of every aspect of life, perseverance has been key to my success. I know and accept that many things will be challenging (writing essays, reading lengthy stories and textbooks), but I have met and can meet these challenges with the tools (instruction and accommodations) that have been provided to me.

At times I have even had to help others understand my learning difference so that proper accommodations could be made. My goal is to be a mechanical engineer and I have been accepted to one of the best engineering universities in the nation – a program that very few "normal" people are accepted to. I would want others facing the same diagnosis as I have know that they, too, can be a success by facing their challenges with a positive attitude and determination. **I would advise them to be very thankful for the diagnosis that they received and understand that this diagnosis will provide them with the appropriate instruction and/or accommodations to be successful.** I would advise the child to be an advocate for himself/herself and share their struggles with their teachers and parents, so that proper assistance can be provided when needed. I would want a child, recently diagnosed with a learning difference, through my experiences and words of advice to feel a message of hope – that they, too, can be very successful – despite their learning differences.

3

I was diagnosed with Cerebral Palsy when I was three years old. At that age, I didn't realize I was any different from my friends. It wasn't until I started school that I began to realize there was a difference between myself and the other kids. I had a speech impediment, had to wear a brace and already experienced two surgeries with three more in my future.

If you are a special child that is challenged by either a physical or learning impediment, this would be my advice to you. Believe in yourself and even though it's hurtful when others make fun of you or tease you, remember to stay strong and don't lower yourself to their level. A lot of the time they tease you simply because they don't understand what it is that makes you unique. Don't let this discourage you.

Stay positive, things will get better. You have to go with the flow. You will have good days and bad days, just like everyone else.

Dealing with bullies can be tricky. Stick up for yourself if possible, but remember that you can always ask a teacher or another adult for help. Bullying is not something adults take lightly, and they will be more than happy to help you. Talking about the problem is a much better solution than ignoring it.

Not everyone will treat you differently. Sometimes you'll meet a very good friend. Someone who looks past your challenges and gets to know you for you. These are the kind of people you want to surround yourself with.

When I was in elementary school, I got made fun of all the time, but there were two girls in my class that weren't going to let the other kids influence their opinions and got to know me. We stayed best friends for years. They were always there for me, and I was there for them, too.

Some of us have more to overcome than others, and that makes you unique.

As you get older, more people will see how good of a person you are. In life there will always be someone who tries to put you down to build themselves up, but as long as you feel confident in the type of person you are, you'll be fine. Having a positive attitude will often change the attitudes of the people around you. Every day will bring challenges, and you'll have some victories and some defeats, but keep looking forward; you never know what tomorrow will bring.

IF YOU ARE A GOOD PERSON,
GOOD THINGS WILL FOLLOW YOU.

NOTICE SMALL KINDNESSES
THAT YOU FIND YOURSELF DOING
AND
OTHER PEOPLE ARE DOING,

AND CONSTANTLY REMIND YOURSELF
OF THE THINGS FOR WHICH YOU'RE GRATEFUL.

LEARNING DIFFERENCES ARE NOT BAD, BUT INSTEAD JUST ANOTHER PART OF WHAT MAKES US ALL HUMAN BEINGS.

I KNOW WHEN I WAS DIAGNOSED I COULD NOT REALLY UNDERSTAND WHAT IT MEANT.

I THOUGHT I WAS NOT AS SMART AS THE OTHER CHILDREN AND THAT I WAS ALWAYS GOING TO BE BEHIND IN SCHOOL.

OF COURSE THIS WAS NOT TRUE, BUT I HAD TO FIGURE IT OUT MYSELF.

4

My battle began at age seven, in the 2nd grade. During a conference my teacher informed my parents that I was lazy, failed to apply myself, and was in jeopardy of not being promoted. My parents had me tested, and found that I was both dyslexic and dysgraphic. All through elementary school, I was in the minority. I attended a local university for reading lessons, and consulted numerous specialists to conquer my disabilities. However, the hard work paid off.

In the fifth grade, I became daring and applied to the Academically and Intelligently Gifted program. This was a huge step. If accepted, I would be placed in more rigorous courses for the remainder of elementary school and the entirety of middle school. Once again, naysayers came knocking; arguing that students couldn't be both academically gifted and learning disabled. They challenged my parents and I stating that I couldn't academically qualify or handle the workload. However, by developing a regimen of study habits, reading lessons, and occupational therapy, I proved them wrong. Not only did I pass the entrance exams, but I made straight "A's" in the more rigorous classes. By the time I entered high school, I was ready to take advanced placement courses for college.

If I were sharing advice with those recently diagnosed with a learning difference, I would tell them to remember not to let the difference own or define them. Dyslexia and Dysgraphia are part of who they are and not something they will be able to change.

They may not bubble correctly on a standardized test, take notes by hand at the same speed as classmates, or read as quickly. But by owning their learning differences and utilizing technology, they can circle correct answers on a test, take excellent notes on a computer, and listen to books on tape. The greater portions of their Being are the lessons learned and skills acquired from learning to manage the differences.

Being dyslexic and dysgraphic is both a burden and a blessing. It has taught me to persevere, and never settle for what others believe you can't achieve.

I am entering college with the study skills of a graduate student, a clear cut map of my career and the understanding that accomplished teachers and real friends are non-judgmental. I enjoy serving my community through various clubs and organizations. My favorite volunteer activity is assisting with the children's summer reading program at our public library.

I would like to tell all children with learning differences to never settle for what others think they should achieve, always dream that you can do more, and believe in your ability to create your dreams though sweat, determination, and hard work.

5

Take my word for it, having an LD is not as bad as it seems. I remember when my mother told me that I, myself, have Triple X Syndrome. The name was foreign, yet everything, all the signs, seemed to show me otherwise. Now it made sense, all the trouble I had in school was due to this. I didn't really know how to take the news at first, so I let my parents guide me all the way. If you are also fortunate enough to have parents who are as dedicated to helping you succeed, then you can reach your potential. However, it takes participation on your part too. You should know ahead of time, you won't be 'fixed' with the snap of your fingers, it takes times and effort. It took me years of working with speech, reading, and writing tutors to improve my learning skills.

You also need the drive and determination to succeed. If you're not driven to help yourself, then nothing will truly be accomplished.

The aid of your parents, tutors, and teachers will mean nothing if you, yourself, don't have the motivation or confidence that you can get to that special place; the place where you are satisfied with how hard you tried and no one could tell you otherwise. I feel that I have personally strived to be the best I could be. I've had my eyes set on my personal goal of being an A student and getting into college without any waivers, and unless someone was notified of my disability, a teacher for example, no one could realize that I have Triple X. All this is because of the tremendous amount of help I've received, and for that I'll always be grateful. Just know that if you preserve, you can get anything you want. Set a challenging goal, and strive for it. **I believe in you.**

6

"Veni Vidi, Vici" was written by Julius Caesar in 47 BC. It is a Latin phrase that means **I came, I saw, I conquered**. This phrase has been a goal of mine since my diagnosis of dysgraphia and ADD.

If you are newly diagnosed with a learning challenging, I would recommend having a PP&Q. A PP&Q means People, Purpose and a Quote.

I was diagnosed later in my childhood. I was almost 14 when I heard news that would change my life. All I heard was learning disability and special education. Those words haunted me for days. I kept hearing them over and over in my head. I didn't want to be labeled as a special education student. I was a normal kid from a normal family. This couldn't be happening to me.

Luckily, I was surrounded with people who wanted to build me up and would not allow me to settle for a label. My parents were as shocked as I was about my diagnosis of dysgraphia. The first words out of my mother's mouth were "Okay, we know what is causing it now, so what are you going to do about it?" I was never allowed to use my learning difference as an excuse. When the special education counselor suggested to my mom that I take an easier road in high school courses and take study skills, she quickly replied with a polite "No Thank You!" The summer prior to my freshman year in high school my mom and I read everything we could find about dysgraphia. We learned so much. It was great to read about successful adults with the problem.

When I got to high school, I had a few accommodations but I tried to only use them when I needed them. I didn't want them to become a crutch. I learned to talk to my teachers and explain what dysgraphia was. It was strange, many of them had never heard of my challenge and it was like I was teaching them. Most of my teachers were supportive and helpful.

If you are diagnosed with a learning difference, you need PEOPLE. People, who will push you, yet understand. You need people who will challenge your educational goals and push you to your limits. You also need people who will understand when you need to ask for help and not look at it as a sign of weakness. I am not saying it has been easy. I'll be flat out honest, it's been hard but it is worth it. My GPA may not be as high as some of my non learning challenged friends, but I know I took courses that challenged me and have prepared me for my future.

People is my first P in PP&Q, and PURPOSE is the next P. Even though you may be learning challenged, you are still very much a part of your school. You have to feel that you belong; you have to have a purpose to be at school other than just class. I found out quickly that my passion for band, varsity swimming and Model United Nations kept me going. If I was frustrated with a class, teacher, or assignment, I knew that I had to keep my grades up so I could do the extracurricular activities I loved. I also found that while I was involved in these very different organizations, I always seemed to have a team member, band member, or friend in my classes. My purpose was to be the best student I could be. I would suggest that you find your purpose and stay true to that purpose.

Finally, Q is quote. "*Veni, vidi, vici*" is my QUOTE. It is written on my bedroom mirror. It is embroidered on my swim bag. When I turn on my phone, it is my home screen picture. The Latin phrase is important to me because it incorporates my passion of history, while reminding me of those tough Latin I and II classes I took when others thought I should pass it by. I tend to translate the quote a little differently. I CAME to school and had problems. I SAW what was causing the problems after testing and support from my family and teachers while finding a purpose. I CONQUERED high school. Well, not yet, but I am close. Find your PP&Q. Don't expect it to be easy. Remember you too can conquer your goals.

7

I was diagnosed with a Non-Verbal learning disability and ADHD when I was in the second grade. At first I was embarrassed because it made me different from everyone else. Sometimes other kids would get mad at me because I got special help with my work and test. It was hard to accept the fact that I was different than my friends and classmates, and that I had to learn different. I am a senior now, and over the years I have learned how to help myself. I try not to get frustrated at myself when I do not understand something. If you are stressing, it just makes the confusion worse so just take breaks and give your brain time to process what you need to do. This makes standardized tests more difficult for us than it is for other students. I have to go back and read something several times before I can understand what it says, but I have learned that is okay.

Learn to use your accommodations and how to teach yourself things so that you can understand. When graphing is involved in math, I use colored pencils to keep my lines and point separate. When you have to read a passage or book it is okay to read it quietly out load to yourself or ask the teacher to go to the library or out in the hall. Also, try to avoid sitting by your friends in class that you have together, because you will not get as distracted that way. I know that sounds impossible, but it is easier than you think. You are going to want to ask you teacher for printed notes and if the classroom book comes with a tape. You are going to want it use them. If any book comes with audio aid get it and listen to the book as you read it. That will help you understand more.

I know it may be hard to read a person's body language and hard to understand sarcasm. If you are not sure if a person is serious or just joking, around ask them. One of the most important things I have learned is it is okay to ask questions if you do not understand something. Don't be embarrassed because someone else in your class may have the same question. Probably the most important thing you can do is just believe in yourself. If you do not understand something keep on trying until you do. I know it gets frustrating, but just relax and just remember that you can do it.

8

Pride. The hamartia of the Greek heroes. When damaged, it can lead to irrational rage. Or it can beget determination. When I was twelve, my father explained that my goals were out of reach. He expounded that few people survive in upper level classes, and I was not one of them. After their divorce, I was fighting my mother's high academic expectations. One would think telling me this would reinforce my anti-homework beliefs. Unfortunately for my dad, his words had the opposite effect. I vowed to exceed his expectations. Two diagnoses and five years later, I took psychology to better understand my learning disabilities. Thus far, I hypothesize that I lack a functional right cerebral cortex, and due to my mind's plasticity, I now have an inhumanly amazing left hemisphere.

My teacher conducted tests to confirm the diagnosis born from my brain pondering itself (brainception!). I have a true lack of visual memory. I do not think in pictures, only in words. Show me a picture of a flower and I can commit to memory that it is red or beautiful, but I cannot visualize it. I cannot remember what my mother's face looks like, or even my own. This makes my processing speed very slow. If I want to learn something, I must commit it to my long-term memory.

I must work twice as hard as the other students to learn the same material. After years of studying until 2 AM, I finally found academic success. Because of my learning disability, I must actually understand the information in order to learn, using the educational system for its true purpose. Language functions, such as grammar and vocabulary, are based in the left hemisphere, proved objectively by my perfect score of 800 in critical reading on the SAT exam.

Did I succeed in spite of my disabilities or because of them? At the age of seven, I was taking a timed standardized test required by "No Child Left Behind." I needed to go to the restroom, and washed my hands. An hour later I returned, thinking five minutes had elapsed. My teacher was angry because I missed most of the exam, and it seemed I would indeed be left behind. I can remember being fascinated by the water as I washed my hands, mesmerized by the sounds of the water splashing, the feeling of cold, the sight of a rainbow of colors in my tiny cupped palms. Water was alive with possibilities, but filling in a standardized test with a number two pencil was mundane.

As I aged, I became tired of being the girl with her head in the clouds, and decided instead to become the smart girl. But achieving this goal has not always been easy. It takes time for me to comprehend and process jokes. I am always a split second too late with a comeback, so I often remain silent. But inside my mind, I make connections others do not. I volunteer to create a playground for the less fortunate children in my neighborhood, and I am the one who thinks to paint a princess and a knight around the ovals in the door, so the kids can put their faces in the hole and imagine a better life where they are the queens and kings. My whole perspective on life shifted when I realized my disability could make me a better student. It brought me higher up the mountain, so I could see how everything fit together below. I found clarity.

Isn't that what we all strive for in life? I just finished applying to some of the most prestigious universities in the United States, and my top 1% class rank and 99.5% standard aptitude test scores place me above the mean of currently attending freshmen. I plan to study bioengineering, and eventually attend medical school as the fourth generation to do so in my family. I have no doubt I will achieve this goal. To understand me, one must understand how high knowledge is on my list of life's priorities.

The key to success in life is to be prepared for any situation, and the only way to be prepared is to have as much knowledge as possible.

With knowledge comes respect, which I crave, especially from my father. I must beat the odds, always working harder than everyone else if I want others to acknowledge my intelligence. An intelligence of which I am immensely proud.

I have been characterized as disabled student by my public high school. I have been tested for hours and given diagnoses of ADHD, distracted type, with a slow processing speed and the largest differential between IQ and information processing speed that the psychologist with twenty years experience had ever seen. When I was first diagnosed, I was embarrassed to be singled out during exams. I needed extra time, and the teacher would frequently announce it in front of the entire class. Even worse, during the untimed state mandated standardized tests, the teacher would announce that one student still had not finished, and the entire class would turn and look at me, silently pressuring me to work faster. I had some teachers who implied I was intentionally working slowly, as if anyone would desire to be the slowest student in the class. My advice to a newly diagnosed disabled student is to believe in yourself, and understand that no matter what your disability is, you can still be the hardest working student in your class. Maximize your potential, be determined, and set your sights high, because no label should limit what is possible for your future. **Be proud!**

OVER THE YEARS I HAVE HAD TO WORK HARDER THAN MOST STUDENTS, BUT THIS HAS TAUGHT ME PATIENCE, DETERMINATION AND PERSISTENCE.

FACING MY CHALLENGES HAS ALSO TAUGHT ME HOW TO BE PERCEPTIVE AND EMPATHETIC TOWARDS OTHERS.

9

"You are going to be ok" would be the first thing I would tell a child newly diagnosed with a learning difference. I would tell them to talk about their learning disability – they will find they aren't the only one who has had to struggle. Being different is not bad and there are a lot of things you could have been born with that would make your life more difficult than a learning disability.

I would tell them to ask for help when they need it and that sometimes getting help won't be easy. When I was in elementary school they really focused on getting us to be advocates for ourselves starting when we were in grade school. I was glad they had done that because I had to use some of the skills they gave me when I was having trouble in my AP World History class in high school. When we were grading tests, the teacher read the answers so fast I couldn't keep up. When he lectured, he NEVER wrote anything down. I finally had to go see him (I put it off too long so another piece of advice I have is not to wait!) and when I told him I was struggling because of my learning disability he said there was no such thing as either a learning disability or ADHD. I just kept talking to him and by the end of our meeting he was helping me with college choices – sometimes you just have to keep trying. You have to learn how to succeed in different situations and this was just one more of those. I made it through the course and the experience actually made me more confident about approaching teachers when I was struggling which I will need to be able to do in college.

Another piece of advice I would give the child is that if they can qualify for help, like extended time on tests, taking it and take it as soon as they can get it. I didn't get it because I was doing okay in school and I didn't want anyone to think I was dumb and then I needed it for college testing and it was hard to get. Taking the ACT and SAT is much easier with a learning disability if you have extra time.

I would advise this child to be open with teachers because most of them will help them with whatever they need but I would not advise them to tell their coaches if they are in sports. I play baseball and there have been times I have missed the signs because of my auditory processing learning disability. I think most of my coaches would say my learning disability was an excuse so sometimes I am yelled at and I just try harder and I guess that works for me. I would like to tell this child that everyone will understand and help you but I have not found that always to be true.

I would tell the child to try a lot of different things that they enjoy and find something they do well. I tried a lot of sports and decided baseball was the right one for me which helped my confidence. I made a lot of friends who like me for who I am and what I do for the team. They don't care if I have a learning disability although if I forget to take my ADHD medication they can tell – I am much more entertaining without it but I know I need it to focus!

When the child picks schools to attend, I would tell them to pick one where they will have the best chance of success, not the one all of their friends want to go to. I went to one for first and second grades where they really helped me. Then I went to another school where I had small enough classes that they noticed if I was having trouble with a class. After the 8th grade I really wanted to go to a bigger school. My parents were not sure that was the right decision for me but finally agreed to let me try. Since I am on track to graduate, I guess I made it work but if you have a learning disability you have to be really careful about making sure you can succeed in larger classes and without teachers who really understand how you learn best. You will also need to think about that when they go to college.

Finally, I would tell a child with a learning disability to surround themselves with people who will encourage them. Grandparents, parents, friends, teachers, counselors, coaches – whoever is in their lives that will be positive about them just the way they are. Being "different" doesn't mean I am not as good as any "normal" person. And I would tell that child to never, never, never give up – they will be just fine!

I AM …….IN THE BOY SCOUTS AND IN ROBOTICS CLUB AT SCHOOL.

NEXT YEAR, I WILL BE PLAYING FOOTBALL AT COLLEGE.

I TAKE AN ADVANCED PHOTOGRAPHY COURSE AND HAVE MY OWN PHOTOGRAPHY BUSINESS.

I PLAY IN JUNIOR GOLF TOURNAMENTS.

I ENJOY PARTICIPATING IN ART CLASSES, DRAMA CLUB, FRENCH CLUB, ART CLUB AND KEY CLUB.

I ENJOY VOLUNTEER WORK AND HAVE SPENT OVER 100 HOURS TAKING APART COMPUTERS.

10

One of the hardest things about school is not the material but rather the atmosphere set up by my peers. Many students at my school and kids my age believe that the end goal is not growing in your knowledge or even the grades; the ultimate sign of success is doing well while only putting forth minimal effort. I cringe every time my neighbor declares they're dyslexic because they switched up some numbers in math.

Paralyzed by the thought of exposing my secret, I stood by while one of my more ill-tempered friends ranted that a particular boy had to have cheated on an essay because there was no conceivable way this challenged boy could write anything better than her. This boy is the single person at my school that I know also struggles with a learning disability. People make comments mocking his chicken starch writing and discredit his gift in math by highlighting his shortcomings in Language Arts. He isn't the best human being on the planet, but I defend him all the same because I understand how trying school can be when you have been trained to be ashamed of how you think.

All people are self-conscious about aspects of themselves, but flaws are generally only skin deep. The struggle with self-presentation is at the core of us and this struggle unites us.

For some reason we have an unspoken bond that goes deeper than our shared way to awkwardly hold a pencil. His dysgraphia, like my speech impediment, serve as a constant reminder of his lack of control and our flaws we can't hide. There comes a point where you simply can't decide if it's better to accept the way things are or continue to fight yourself at every turn.

11

Throughout my entire life I've been told by teachers, doctors, and peers that I will never be able to do the same things that other people can do; that I was going to be constantly held back by my condition. However I wasn't going let that happen. I pushed myself, that no matter what I had; despite my physical or mental condition, I would not let it get in my way. I would push myself to be like everyone else, as if nothing was wrong with me. But it doesn't always work out like that every day.

I wake up every morning forgetting something that I did before, because I have short-term memory loss due to a bran arachnoid cyst I was born with and was removed when I was 8. I don't always remember names, just have ask my friends, I sometimes forget theirs. I also have physical pains like a 90-year-old man while I'm only 18 years old and in my prime; Another side effect is having fevers so bad (105 to 107) that I become immobile and have to be rushed to the emergency room to do extreme testing to make the pain subside. They still have not been able to diagnose me even after 18 years of seeing the best doctors at my local hospital and a national hospital.

I have had these pains since I was a baby; my mom says one of my first words was "beeping" while pointing to my head. We found out later it was migraines. I would stop walking at times and found out later it was because of my joint and muscle pain but I didn't know how to say it so I just stopped walking. At 2 ½ they thought I had leukemia because of my lab work, but that wasn't it. I have never had a day without pain so I don't know how that feels. At age 9 one of my doctors determined there was nothing they could do and I would have to live this way and work this way. At that time I had missed weeks of school due to my fevers and pain, but I told my mom I wanted to go anyway and went half days until I could go back to full days. That episode lasted 3 years.

I am now waiting to see if I will be accepted in the undiagnosed department at my children's hospital so my parents can have some peace of mind just knowing what I have so I can get the care I need and the medicine I need for the joint and muscle pain. I am in remission now but I never know when "it" will hit me. I can't afford to miss school because it takes me weeks to catch up.

Despite it all, I know I'm blessed, I know that many others are worse off than me, and my prayers go out to them every night. That is one of the many reasons why I had my Boy Scout Eagle Scout project benefit my local children's hospital. The blankets that I made are there to comfort the children that don't have someone to hold them. I want them to know that someone is always praying and thinking of them; I know that some of them won't make it back home from the hospital. I received one of these blankets when I had brain surgery. I still have it today.

I feel extremely blessed because I made it back from the hospital. I'm still able to be here on this earth, and have a will to spread His word, my word and the word of many other people to never give up! To never let something that's holding them down, keep them there, but to be successful and happy no matter what you have holding you down. To break away from those chains, and do something other than blaming what's setting you back, and to strive forward.

In school, I was told that I was not a good candidate for Advanced Placement (AP) courses due to all my learning obstacles but when I started middle school, I was determined to succeed in AP courses. As a freshman at my high school, I was awarded "Most Outstanding English Student" and "Most Outstanding Science student"; I have also been named a Senior Patrol Leader of my Boy Scout troop.

These things don't come easy for me. I have to work twice as hard and twice as long as other students. I am up for hours just to do homework because I can't remember how to sometimes even do the work because I already forgot by the time I get home.

Personally, some days when I'm at the hospital unable to move and with no one around but the nurses and doctors poking and prodding at me; being told over and over again that you just can't do it, and you're always going to be like this, I could have given up hope. But then I think of all the people in my life; all the people that have supported me in all these difficulties and challenges. They believed in me, even when I couldn't believe in myself. They were the ones that helped me to pick myself up and push me on even if I couldn't do it myself. They are the reason I am still here today.

I am truly blessed to be recognized for my abilities and not for my disabilities.

Now, take the time to think of yourself. Do you have any chains? Do you have anything that's holding you down; and if you do how can you overcome it? Who is going to hold you up when you can't do it yourself, and who's going to be there no matter what happens? Because if you try and do it by yourself and you fail, what happens then, what are you going to do after that happens? Just give up? Or just go back and try the same thing for the same outcome. I'm telling you to go out and find help. You may not think anyone's there to help you but someone's always waiting someone is always there to help you through your toughest times, you just have to find them. I have!

12

If I were to speak to someone that was newly diagnosed with learning disabilities, I would willingly share my journey and let them know that you can come out on the other side. Nobody would ever choose to struggle but in the end facing and overcoming challenges can actually be very rewarding in itself.

I think the hardest part of having hidden disabilities like dyslexia, dysgraphia, ADHD (inattentive), processing, executive function concerns and short term memory deficits is that people tend to negate your struggle.

There is definitely a lack of compassion, and people think your accommodations are unnecessary and give you an advantage over you classmates. I wanted to badly to fit in and do well in school and it just was always out of reach and the gap widened as the years progressed. In grade school, teachers were quick to label me as lazy. I knew I was bright or at least I thought I was pretty smart. Private testing in the third grade finally began to unravel the mystery. But this point, however, my self-esteem had taken a pretty regular beating from teachers who were unwilling to acknowledge there even was a problem.

The one piece of advice I would give to a child or probably more importantly to the part of a child struggling is that you need to drop your pride and keep searching for the door that unlocks your child's future.

It is very easy to accept surface reasoning as to why your child is not doing well in school. In the short term, you may believe nothing is wrong, or not want a label. The truth is you can't go to battle unless you know what you are fighting.

I overheard my Mom just this week counseling a friend whose child is just starting the testing and identification process. She told her something that she has parroted to me many times over the years. You cannot have a learning disability unless there is a discrepancy between your IQ and your output. If you have a low IQ and your output is marginal, there is sadly nothing that can be done.

Yes, I struggled with a lot of things growing up and in all honesty, I still do. My processing and short term memory issues impact me socially. I have a very hard time keeping up in fast moving peer to peer conversations. This is something that I am working on right now utilizing ABA Therapy. I know because I am now on the other side of the battle that life really is all about your journey. There was a time not long ago where my future was nowhere near this bright. I always dreamed of going to college, but that was never guaranteed.

I was the first of my friends accepted last year to the National Honor Society. My Mom sat there sobbing because she was sure that I was the only one up there who was, on this day, in her words, "rocking an IEP".

I don't have the luxury of just jumping in head first, but with planning and some supports I will succeed. I have a proven track record of climbing much tougher terrain and knowing that gives me confidence to forge on. The biggest problem I have right now is deciding which of my choices I am planning to pursue. This I have to tell you is a wonderful problem with which to struggle and I do so with a smile on my face and a real sense of accomplishment and pride in my heart.

13

I wish there was a different word other than "diagnosis".

It was an interesting time in my life when the "official word" came down. I was 12 years old when I was diagnosed with a laundry list of disorders that I could not even pronounce. It was shocking. It was overwhelming. It was confusing. It was a relief.

It would have been wonderful to have a peer offer advice to me back them. Here is what I would like to have heard:

Take a deep breath. Don't panic. This is not a bad thing.

In some ways a diagnosis is almost like getting a "do-over". Now that everyone has all (or most of) the facts the journey begins anew... but with a new set of rules.

Keep in mind that this is YOUR journey. It begins with a single step onto the path that you will travel for the rest of your life. There is much to learn along the way.

Knowing how your brain works is a really good thing. If you can name it... you can tame it!

Do not be discouraged when you encounter step hills and sharp curves. Some things will always be hard for you to do and there will always be people who just don't "get-it". Don't let it keep you down.

Enjoy the journey. Marvel at your successes along the way and try to maintain a sense of humor. My personal dyslexic theme song is "Anything you can do I can do backwards".

The fact of the matter is that everybody learns differently. Who you are does not change when a "diagnosis" is attached to the way that you learn.

You are special... but you have always known that. What you may not realize just yet is that you are in good company.

HOW DO YOU GET TO THE TOP?
YOU SEEK HELP AND YOU BELIEVE IN
YOURSELF.

I THINK THAT HAVING TO LEARN TO
TO FOCUS, WORK HARD
AND TO BELIEVE IN MYSELF
HAVE BENEFITTED MY LIFE.

LEARN TO STAND UP FOR YOURSELF. THEY
CALL THIS SELF-ADVOCATING.

IF YOU BELIEVE THAT A CERTAIN TYPE OF
ACCOMMODATION WILL HELP YOU DEAL WITH
A LEARNING PROBLEM, ASK FOR IT.

14

Dear Dyslexic Friend,

You have joined the ranks of people like Orlando Bloom, an actor from *Pirates of the Caribbean* and the *Lord of the Rings*; Alexander Graham Bell, the inventor of the telephone; George S. Patton Jr., a famous general from World War Two; Albert Einstein, E=MC²; Andy Warhol, who famous painter; John F. Kennedy, President of the United States that fought against segregation; Whoopi Goldberg, one of the funniest actresses; Muhammad Ali, the boxer; John Lennon, from the Beatles; Magic Johnson, Los Angeles Lakers basketball player; Richard Branson, space entrepreneur and founder of Virgin Enterprises; F. Scott Fitzgerald, author of <u>The Great Gatsby</u>; Winston Churchill, the most famous Prime Minister of England; and me, to name a few.

Congratulations! You have a gift. Many people will call your gift a disability, but you are not disabled.

You just cannot do some things that people think you should be able to do, but that is okay. Albert Einstein could not speak until the age of nine and never really learned to tie his shoes; he still went on to be the most famous scientist of the 20th Century. You can see the world differently than everyone else. As a dyslexic, I have learned to cope with the hard parts of my dyslexia and developed some tips. Here they are:

WORK! The hard side of dyslexia is that you will struggle in school. You will have to work harder than anyone around you. When you do this, the reward will be immense. Do not use your dyslexia as a crutch for laziness. I normally take about three times as long as other students on most assignments, and I could not read until ninth grade; but I kept on working.

Build a network and community that can support you through your journey. Most people like to help; take advantage of this. Build a community of teachers, family and friends that are aware of your different way of thinking and are supportive. I have been very fortunate. My parents and teachers have worked extremely hard to help me overcome my disabilities.

Advocate for yourself and other dyslexics. There are a lot of misconceptions about dyslexia. These misconceptions can be corrected. Even though you are young you have more authority about yourself and your needs than anyone else does.

Experiment. I joke that I learned the alphabet in four different methods and still need to sing it every time I look someone up in a telephone book. Your first learning program may not overcome your disability; so try again. If something is not working for you, find something else. For a while, I tried taking pictures of the school whiteboard to capture my homework assignments. However this did not work, because I did not have enough time between classes to capture the image, if there was an image, and most of the time I forgot to take the phone, anyway. Instead, I use our school's computer-based grading system to keep up on what's due.

Find a passion that you love and you are good at; then actively pursue it. As a dyslexic, you will find that things other people do with ease, may be very difficult for you. You will also find that you have other gifts. These gifts may be anything from opera singing to carpentry. If you have a passion, it will be much easier to deal with the difficult aspects of your dyslexia. My passion is dance, and I focus much of my life on it. My dance has the added benefit of activating my brain in ways that help mitigate my dyslexia.

The most important thing to remember is that you are human. You do have a learning disability, but don't let it define you. Enjoy your life, share your gift and work hard with what you have.

15

Excuses for a teenager are like snow in the winter. We always use them to try to get out of difficult situations or problems that we face. Excuses related to school are likely the most common. One example would be, "Everyone in the class cheated so I wasn't the only one." As students we too often fall into the trap of blaming others or forming excuses whenever possible. Having a learning disability can be used the same way, but this does not have to be the case.

When I found out I was dyslexic, I was relieved to discover the reason for my reading struggles.

At the same time, I did not want to succumb to using a learning disability as an excuse to not try or to not challenge myself with advanced classes. Some of the accommodations you may receive for this disability are extra time on tests, or receiving a copy of the teacher's notes for subjects requiring a lot of note taking. I strongly suggest using these tools to help further your success in the classroom and to allow you to keep up with your peers. By sucking up my pride and using these accommodations, I have succeed in the classroom, and to date, I have earned just over a 4.0 GPA in high school.

Having a learning disability can be seen as a negative to most people, but I view it as a positive. I feel that we, the learning disabled, are special and unique in our own way.

Students with learning disabilities need to understand that even if it takes us longer to learn something, being able to work harder to gain knowledge helps us develop a good work ethic.

This will serve you well into the future because having a good work ethic will take you farther in life than natural ability alone ever will.

I would also encourage you to realize that you are in good company. There are many famous people with learning disabilities that have occupations spanning from: artists, writers, professional sports players, doctors, scientists, and political leaders. A few of these well known people include:

Pablo Picasso, Steven Spielberg, Magic Johnson, Agatha Christie, John F. Kennedy, and Thomas Edison. Knowing the contributions these people have made spurs me on to live up to my full potential.

I have never met a person who did not have at least one weakness.

Being aware of mine actually helps me to not use it as an excuse but to turn it into a strength. You can turn your learning differences into a strength too when you decide not to use it as an excuse to not learn or to not try. Use the accommodations that you are entitled to so you can become the best student you are capable of being. Finally, be motivated by the famous people who have made tremendous contributions despite the fact they had to overcome a learning disability.

16

Having differences is what makes us unique – even learning differences. They are not an excuse for lack of effort, but rather an explanation of an individual's learning style. The key is to form a toolbox that is filled with tools needed to build a sturdy learning foundation. There is no magical collection of tools that will help you succeed, because your toolbox is unique to you. You must work hard and with your family and teachers to collaborate a learning system for you.

My story begins in second grade, when I was diagnosed with dyslexia. For the next four years, my reading coach and I fashioned a toolbox filled with life tools.

Three of the most important tools were my hammer, nails, and level. The hammer was my voice, pounding endlessly with questions until the nails were firmly secure in my learning foundation. The nails were the lessons that help hold my foundation together. The level kept me balanced in my pursuit of knowledge. These three tools created a sturdy foundation that grows stronger daily.

Hard work, patience, and determination, along with expert guidance from learning specialists, are some of the major tools to building success.

17

When my parents set me down and told me I had dyslexia, I cried for a long time. After coming to a partial understanding of my diagnosis, I was better off. When this happened, I was about 8 years old and still did not have a complete understanding what this news meant. It took a few years for me to see how this would affect my life. My goal in life has been to help people in my situation.

My advice to a child with dyslexia is that you are a smart child; you just have to find a different way to retain the information. Repeat after me, "I am a smart child." That is what you have to tell yourself every time you want to give up. You have to find a way to learn your material that works best for you. Many students in our situation have found that repetition is the best way to learn. This means that they learn the material best by seeing it, saying it, hearing it and writing it. Once again you have to find a way that works for you.

I have found that having a learning disability is a road block, but a road block with detours.

People can tell you how they think you should learn, but you are the only person that can figure out how to get around this road block. For me, getting around this road block is using flashcards, color coding things, rewriting out my notes, and asking a lot of questions. This method is all about trial and error. The only way you will find out what works for you, is to try something and fail at it. It is proven that if you don't succeed at something the first time, the second time you try it, you will have a better success rate.

I did not let my learning disability define my life. I defined my life. Every time I thought about giving up, quitting or letting myself down, I STOPPED and thought, "What would Mia Hamm say?" I have been playing sports ever since I could walk. My parents put me on a soccer team at the age of three and I have been playing sever since then. Being around the world of sports, you find yourself looking up to professional athletes that you want to be like. Mia Hamm has not only inspired me to be the best athlete I can be, she inspired me to be the best student I can be. That is what leads me to one of her famous quotes, "I've worked too hard and too long to let anything stand in the way of my goals. I will not let my teammates down and I will not let myself down." I have made a promise to myself that I will never give up no matter what the situation is. I have found through the course of my life that I am me, a daughter, an athlete, a person who is proud to say "Yes I do have a learning disability and it has taught me to live my life the way I do. Always be positive and never give up." If you follow my advice you will have a lot of success in your future!

Never give up! That is what I have learned from many years of sports. When times get hard, that is when you have to push yourself to the next level.

You have to be willing to put in the time needed to reach your goals. There are no magic fairies out there to spread pixie dust on you to make you successful. To reach for the stars means you are going to need to invest a lot of time and effort into your education to get there. I know how frustrating it is when you are reading something and not understanding it. We, as humans, read a lot in a day. Having a learning disability that involves reading problems can be hard. Everywhere you go there is something you have to read. I have found that if you just clear you mind a few minutes and continue with your work, you will be successful. The harder you work, the better you will be in the future.

The first day of classes every year, I walk up to my teachers and introduce myself. In this conversation, I explain to them that I am on a 504, or sometimes called an IEP. I have found with these conversations that if you are willing to put the time and effort into a teacher's class, they will make sure you succeed.

Within this conversation, we usually talk about outside materials I can use to make my life easier. These are not easy conversations to have, but they need to be done. I guarantee you, that if you do this, your teachers will have more respect for you than any other student. You hold the code to make your life successful and you have to choose to decode it.

The most important piece of advice I got was from my mom. She is a strong confident woman who cares deeply for me. When we wrote my

504 for the first time she told me, "You will not use your disability as a crutch to get through school. It is just a tool to make you successful."

That advice defined my life in school. I have never misused the accommodations that I was given. I understand that I need to get an education to make my future better and brighter. Don't abuse your rights and you will do amazing in school.

18

Over my 18 years of living I have faced what I would like to think of as a moderate amount of resistance. I would not say that I have had a hard life but it has not been easy. The hardest and I think most life altering struggle is one that I have had to face every day. From the moment I wake up to the moment I fall asleep I face this one challenge. Dyslexia, this is a brain-based type of learning disability that specifically impairs a person's ability to read. Because of this fact, everything involving reading or writing becomes a challenge. Writing essays are a challenge for me. I must type out all my essays using Microsoft Word and have others check them for me. My ability to recognize words is extremely poor, let alone spell them. I overcome this burden by memorizing words not as letters but as pictures because every word is just another picture. I read the English language more like Chinese symbols. Every time I encounter a new word I must look at it many times to imbed it into my brain. When reading, I try and predict the word that is coming next by using context clues, this helps with the flow of my reading. When it comes to reading comprehension I am fantastic because of my high vocabulary. I feel that not only has this disability changed me, but it has changed me for the better. Because of my dyslexia, I have grown stronger in other parts of learning. Now computers help me to overcome any issues with spelling and allow me to reach my full potential.

For those that are also affected by a disability or another hardship, the best thing to tell them is that they can do it. People have a hard time seeing that a person with a learning disability is most times more gifted than their counterparts. The time that is most important for a student like this is, high school. This is a time where you are trying to find who you are.

The best advice I could give them is to never stop work. Things will be harder but, that comes to the ground. Perseverance is important. For my first semester it was hard to get use to the new environment but as soon as you find your feet you must bound ahead. When you run into problems remember to use your counselors and teachers you know. If it wasn't for some really nice teachers at my school I might have never even made it. Teachers will always be ready to help those in need. Getting to know yourself is the next step.

If you do not know yourself you will never know anyone else.

As long as you try and never give up on your work you will do fine in class. Never be afraid to tell a teacher what you need help for. They want to help you.

19

People have asked me what it was like when I was officially told I had dyslexia. I always tell them: it's like being told you're broken.

It feels like someone has just told you that you don't match the standards of society. That you are a weak link and something is seriously wrong with you. The process itself is rather disheartening, someone who barely knows you is sitting across a large desk, while their degrees look down at you as if they are laughing, while he or she talks about all these problems you have and how messed up you are. I could tell you almost exactly how any kid who's sitting in any psychiatrist office feels; alone, mistreated, abused, defective and guilty.

The way that child is thinking is understandable and completely normal. A major problem with the diagnosis process is that it makes you feel stupid or inadequate. However if such thoughts persists in the child's mind there is not a way that kid is going to "beat" his disability. No matter how much it feels like their psychiatrist is scoffing at their intellect, or how much the process of the diagnosis has made them feel inadequate, a new thought process is needed or that child is never going to be as successful as possible. If the child perceives his disability as a limit to his ability, his intellect or his wealth as a human being that child will be trapped by their disability their while life. The child must change his perception of his diagnosis in order for it not to become a hindrance to their life.

The diagnosis of a learning disability can make even the highest performing kids feel as if he can no longer succeed in their activities outside of school. Yes, the fact the student has a learning disability will make some things in life more difficult but the diagnosis itself doesn't hurt their chances of success. In fact it probably helps, now the child can target problems and figure out a way around them. The child now has a better idea of how he struggles in whatever they are passionate about and can discover better ways to help them succeed. Whether it's a sport, an art craft or an academic club a learning disability has a large effect on the student's ability to perform in said positions. I would tell a recently diagnosed child to turn the diagnosis into a positive by using it to combat the difficulties they have in their extra-curricular activities.

Nothing changed about his intelligence since the diagnosis except for the fact he is now armed with knowledge that can help him improve his brain capacity.

The student could also use the diagnosis to better his intellect. He can now focus on ways in which his learning disability would make his school work more difficult. Instead of sulking in the fact that it is now documented that he has shortcomings in some brain functions, I would encourage students with dyslexia to improve those functions by using the new knowledge to improve his school work.

Another way a diagnosis really affects a child is the fact that their self-confidence or self-worth was greatly affected by the diagnosis. What I would encourage the child to remember is that a diagnosis changed nothing; it just gave him critical information. It doesn't mean they can't be whatever they want to be. Their life's path is not at all altered for the worse. The student needs to be constantly reminded of this in order to avoid falling into the trap of self-pity which only breeds regression. This is the most important thing I would do because without self-confidence the child is going to struggle mentally and emotionally, there's no way around it. These last thing the diagnosis should do is make the child question themselves.

Perception is the most important thing I would stress to anybody recently diagnosed with a learning disability. If they sulk in defeat then he is going to not achieve his full potential, in fact he will regress. But if the child understands that the diagnosis changed nothing at all, it just gave him information then they are more likely to use the diagnosis to their advantage, rather bleak to the child experiencing it.

20

Although difficulties will arise with your dyslexia diagnosis, you have the choice to not only over come, but to soar over "your mountain".

One cannot succeed on his own; outside support will aid in fighting through one's weaknesses and rejoice in one's successes.

So, embrace the struggle. Be the best you.

Like rare jewels, you are precious. Show the world how bright you can shine.

21

In today's society, a tremendous amount of pressure is put on kids to succeed in every aspect of their lives; whether it is in academics, athletics, community service, you name it. However, I feel like in all the trials and tribulations of life, there is one stress that terrifies kids of all ages more than anything, and that's being different. When my parents first informed me about my learning disability and the necessary measures I would need to take in working around it, standing out from my peers terrified me. Instead of embracing the unconventional way my mind worked, I would do every possible thing I could to appear like the "traditional student". I would simply let my confusion and frustrations simmer in school, and put forth no effort to seek out learning strategies best suited for me. It wasn't until right around the time I started high school that I let go of my insecurities and became fully comfortable "in my own head". Implementing this new-found proactive approach to my learning differences led to higher grades, better relationships with my teachers, and an overall better understanding of who I am as a person.

To this day I still regret the many years I spent stressing about classmates perceiving my disorder as stupidity, and not advocating for myself with my teachers. This is why I am so adamant in advising any child who is being diagnosed with a learning difference to take pride in it, and embrace the uniqueness surrounding the way he or she learns.

Take the time to analyze your own scholarly strengths and weaknesses, and organize a blueprint of strategies to ensure life is as stress free as possible for you. Never allow an initial lack of comprehension cause frustration and a pessimistic attitude towards learning. I have an auditory processing disorder, so often times it takes me ten explanations to understand a concept many people grasp in one.

Rather than building up rage and having these setbacks affect my confidence, I became determined to master that concept at a higher level than the person who can get by after a single explanation. As a result of the extra time and effort often times needed with studies, a strong emphasis on time management was a key component of my success.

Learning disabilities make it extremely challenging to cram for tests the night before while still succeeding. I've found that the best approach to studying is to break down chapters into small sections, and review smaller amounts of material each night so you can ask questions leading up to the test.

In order to prevent becoming burnt out and complacent from putting forth so much extra effort, I've found that listing out tangible goals can help one stay on track. They don't all have to be daunting tasks and remarkable achievements, but simple goals such as staying after school and working with the math teacher two times a week.

There is no magical formula, advice, or procedure that can cure you or me of a learning disability. It takes a willingness to open up to learning something new about oneself each day by being prideful, proactive and persistent in regards to the adversities that come our way.

22

I know that look on your face: shock, confusion, and bewilderment. What does this mean? What do I have? Why am I different? Does it make me weird? Normal? I thought all of those things when I was told I have dyslexia. The first thing you need to know is that yes, you are normal. Over 10% of the population has some sort of learning difficulty. The differences that will begin to take effect in your life are normal. You may not take certain math classes or reading classes. You may have an assistant to help you with your school work. You may take classes like everyone else. This will be up to your counselor. If you have perceptual dyslexia, like I do, you have problems with climbing down stairs, reading for long periods of time, absorbing information you have read, and depth perception.

At times it will seem annoying and nauseating, but the best thing to do is just step back, take a few deep breaths, find your focus, and continue on. If you feel too stressed or confused to keep studying or practicing then step away to go relax. Play a video game, sit down, or take a walk. Find a good stress relieving hobby and use that whenever you can't focus. People who are insecure in themselves will always make fun of you. It does not matter if you have a learning difficulty or if you have a strange looking birthmark. They are going to do it so face that fact. Surround yourself with good friends who will uplift you and help you through your difficulties. Just because you have a learning difficulty, does not mean that you cannot achieve you dreams. There are doctors, lawyers, and great men and women who have many different learning difficulties. Use them as your inspiration.

23

Never let anyone, especially teachers, put you down because you have a learning disability.

It doesn't matter what you have. If you decide to succeed, no one can stop you.

Your disability is not just extra heavy weight put on a big stone put on top of you. If you really work at it, you can shape the stone to be your weapon. You can use your other skills to compensate. I have dyslexia. I have a good memory and a good understanding of math. I am now comfortable with myself. You can train your brain to where it's no longer the problem. The real problem with LD is it can make you lazy and you can accept that you can't do things. It's like a drug. You get addicted to it and decide it's who you are. But it's not true if you decide it's not true.

24

If I was counseling a student who had just found out that he/she (he) had a learning difference, I would probably start by telling him that he is not just a student and that he is essentially no different than his classmates. He is just as smart as his classmates; but he will have to work a little harder and a little differently. I would tell him that it took me a long time to realize that about myself and that for me it was (and still is) painful to admit that I am different in some way. I would say "it may take you a while to get used to the idea that you have a learning difference and that is OK." He might be upset, angry, or embarrassed so I would tell him that there are others like him.

I would also let him know that he should use the accommodations that are available to him (like extra time and taking tests in a separate room) because all that does is to put him on an even playing field with everyone else. Other students, like me, manage to take advanced classes and even excel in them by using a few tools and some extra time. I would also suggest that he let his teachers know about the diagnosis because they will understand when he needs extra time or needs advice. If the person is dyslexic with reading and writing difficulties like me, I might say "oral books and spell-checking software will become your best friends, but still read back your work to check for confused works like 'when and went'."

I would tell him that his classmates will notice that, for example, he is absent from the room when tests are given and that eventually they will work out that he is "different". There will be some individuals who will joke about his learning difference, or tease him, or bully him but I would tell him that he should ignore those idiots because they know nothing about his situation. He should take comfort in a few close friends who will understand him and will support him.

I would end up by saying "don't let anyone make you believe that you can't do something because you have a learning difference; prove them wrong! Know that you can do anything as long as you set your mind to it."

25

Having an LD, things may take you longer to learn and some days they may seem simply impossible, but never give up.

Even though reading was hard for me, I always loved books. When the first Harry Potter book came out, all of my friends wanted to read it. I insisted on reading the book too. My mom bought me the book and she would read it to me each night. I couldn't wait to read more of it each night and found it frustrating that I had to wait for her and I couldn't read it on my own. My aunt suggested getting the book on tape. My mom bought the second Harry Potter book and got the audio to go with it. It was great to be able to read the book at home whenever I wanted to. My Special Education teacher in fifth grade suggested that I get a subscription to RFB&D, which is now Learning Ally. My mom has kept my subscription to Learning Ally active so I would have it when I need it. This has helped me be more independent when I was doing my schoolwork at home. In addition to getting audio novels, I am able to get audio textbooks. Some years I needed more audio books than others. I have read countless books over the years and the audio textbooks have helped me when I needed to review class material or prepare for class.

Another important thing that I have learned over the years is how to advocate for myself. I will ask for extra time on tests and quizzes when I feel I need it. I will also question grades on assignments that I feel are not right. I go for extra help when I need to and always ask for clarification on something if I am not sure.

When I start a new class, I get a feel for what it will be like and prepare myself for it the best I can. Whether it is reviewing material the night before or reading ahead in the book so I know what to expect. I never let my learning disability get in the way of accomplishing something I set my mind to and neither should you. I have always been very involved in many different activities. I love sports. I have been a member of the football team all four years of high school and was the senior captain of the football team this year. I have also been in scouting since I was in first grade. I always knew I wanted to earn my Eagle Scout Rank and last November, I was able to achieve this.

As I move forward through school and adulthood I have learned what I need to do to be successful. I learn differently from some people and it may take me a little longer to accomplish some tasks. I know my strengths and my weaknesses and I will utilize my strengths to be successful. These are some of the most important things that someone with a learning disability needs to learn about him or herself. Remember to work hard, learn your strengths, and learn to advocate for yourself.

Do not let your learning disability get in the way of reaching your goals.

26

"Runners to your mark... set... BANG!!!" All 200 runners sprint off the starting line and the cross country race is underway. This moment is one of the most stressful in sports. As the gun goes off you must immediately look to the future. In many ways running cross country can be related to life. In both running and life the future holds many obstacles; to be successful, a person must set goals and strive to do their best every day.

Much like a cross country course, life has its obstacles. In life the ones who accomplish the most are the ones who are giving it their all. Dyslexia has been one of my obstacles. It has been like a big hill that slows me down. When I face this hill, I must try again and again until I have mastered the obstacle. I work on running up that hill every day and every day I can get to the top faster than before. Soon I will be able to run up that hill faster than anyone else can, until being dyslexic no longer slows me down.

Finishing a race is like completing a chapter in my life; I am proud of what I have accomplished. Then I begin to look forward to the next race in the season or chapter in my life. It is still a challenge like the one I just completed, but this new race/phase will have new obstacles to overcome. For me this next phase is college, and I am confident that my past challenges have trained me to excel in this next course of my life. I look forward especially to the challenges ahead of me in college, because I know it will prepare me for my entire life ahead. No matter how hard I train, I will never truly run a race with perfection, much like I cannot go through life being perfect. Even so, I still strive to unlock my greatest potential every day with the skills I have acquired through hard work. I will always encounter those obstacles that will attempt to hold me up in life, but I will make the best of them by running strong all the way to the finish line.

27

Welcome! Check your anxiety and frustration at the door. You've entered the World of Dyslexia. Here there is a documented, neurological explanation for our war with words. There's a complicated scientific explanation but the bottom line is that our brains work differently than most other peoples. How cool is that?

Membership dues? We have already paid them. We have tried hard. We have concentrated. We have given 100%. We are not lazy. We are dyslexic.

The World of Dyslexia is an intriguing place. It has it challenges. I won't tell you that everything will be easy because it won't be. Now, however, you can understand *why* it is difficult. There are some really amazing discoveries in the World of Dyslexia waiting just for you.

Make a plan! Introduce yourself to you very own, personalized 504 plan. What is that you ask? It's a map that looks at where your challenges are and creates a path to where the resources are that will make learning easier. It will take those mountains, like spelling, punctuation, and really long chapters to read and turn them into hills. Your 504 plan will help you use your strengths to learn the way that works best for you. And guess what? The teachers are in on it! They want you to be successful. They'll follow your plan for you – everyone else gets to learn the old regular way.

Explore! There are a lot of really cool gadgets, devices and software apps out there designed especially to make it easier to learn your way.

I have built some awesome Lego spaceships, fire trucks and castles while listening to an audio book. Spell check is my best friend. Figure out what works for you and, more importantly, figure out what not only works for you but what you're going to use.

Find your voice! For so long you have tried to fly under the proverbial radar. Please, please, teacher, don't call on my. Now you have to learn to speak up for yourself. You're smart, you're trying hard, you just need to be taught the way that your brain learns. Insist that it happens. The boost to your confidence will be enormous. You are your very best advocate.

Use your strengths! Compensate, compensate, compensate. You have been doing this all along; you just probably didn't realize it. You listen intently in class rather than read. I'd bet that you have a great memory. Now you have a word to describe how you've used your strengths to overcome a challenge.

Find yourself a hero! Do a little research. I know that you're really good on a computer. You will be amazed at what dyslexic people have accomplished. They are musicians, innovators, scientists, and athletes. They think and learn differently and succeed where all those ordinary thinkers have failed.

You are about to embark on a journey that will change your life. The World of Dyslexia offers an explanation not an excuse. You have it in you to be successful. Now use that extraordinary brain to show me what you can do!

28

Do you have a LD? You are probably wondering, "How does this change me?" Well, it doesn't.

You are still you and this new label is just one more adjective that you can use to describe yourself. Do not be ashamed… let this new diagnosis be an explanation for the struggles that you have been facing. This difference doesn't simply cause you difficulties however; this is that part of you that is perceptive, creative, and complex. Now that you are aware of your learning difference, you must learn to embrace it.

Relax… there is no need to be embarrassed. You are intelligent and capable in ways unique to you. Maybe the things that your whole class excels at are the things that really challenge you, but don't let that bring you down. Sometimes there will be moments when everyone else is stumped and then it will be your time to shine.

This is why learning differences are often referred to as a gift; because they give people the advantage of a different perspective.

Find the courage to explain to others who you are and what you need. You can't simply expect others to understand you. You must first understand yourself and then help other understand how to help you. It really is okay to ask for assistance, because there will be plenty of times when you will be there to aid others with your specialized talents. Learn to accept the support that many people will be ready to give you. You have what it takes to really grow and succeed, but a little help never hurts.

Enjoy what you are good at. There will always be certain things that remain difficult, but they can often be approached in different ways to make them easier. Figure out how you learn best, because you still do need to learn, and then use that as your very-own-secret-strategy. Don't worry if no one else makes up songs to learn spelling words. If it works for you, do it.

29

When you do face struggles always try, no matter how hard, to forgive yourself. Find within yourself a personal strength or a passion to keep you going. Setting long term goals can help you keep focused and positive. Knowing that you are working toward something that excites you can make the difficulties seem worth it.

People with learning differences always have unique talents. Often they are highly aware of their environment or are very observant and curious. Some of us have a strong sense of creativity and imagination. Many see the Big Picture in the situations around them and in Life. If you can identify where you are the strongest and what feels the best to you, you can embrace it. Leaning into your strengths will really help overcome your weaknesses. Define yourself by what you can do easily, not by what you find hard to do.

My friend, always remember that you are not your label. Your mind is unique and spectacular. If people don't appreciate how amazing you are, show them. Change their attitude about students like you. Be your own advocate and ask for help. Empower others like you to do the same. We need to support one another. Accept your differences and your difficulties, but always remember to let your talents thrive. Make yourself available.

The world needs minds like yours.

30

You define yourself; no one else can do that for you. Even if it feels uncomfortable and you may have to attend a class that not everyone has to go to, remind yourself that it's just a class full of other students facing their own difficulties, don't fight it.

There are teachers who are more than willing to help you with anything. It may be stressful for the first couple weeks but I promise that it will get better.

Take a big breath and jump in – the water is fine.

31

For me, my feelings were mixed when I discovered I had a LD.

On the one hand, I was not happy about having even more things that made me different (I am adopted and have Type 1 diabetes.) But, on the other hand, there was a relief in learning what was wrong and that others struggle with the same things. I began to really understand that I was not alone anymore.

Actually, at my school, I already support students who are recently diagnosed. I reach out especially to those with LD who feel alone and feel like success isn't possible. I listen to their stories, about how they have coped so far.

I tell them: Advocate for yourself. If you don't understand something, talk to your teacher - before school, after classes, whenever they are available. Ask them to explain something again, a different way. Ask for accommodations like more time, or to make assignments shorter. Show your teachers that you are willing to work.

I also let them know that they should let their parents into their lives to help them out; to be patient with their parents because the diagnosis is new for them too.

IF YOU ASK ME, I THINK A DISABILITY HELPS YOU BECOME AN OVER ACHIEVER BECAUSE YOU HAVE TO WORK HARDER THAN OTHERS TO ACCOMPLISH THE SAME TASK.

SOMETHING THAT COMES EASY TO SOMEONE ELSE DOES NOT COME EASY TO US, WHICH CAUSES US TO BUILD A STRONGER STAMINA THAN OTHERS.

IF YOU HAVE ADHD, SCHOOL CAN FEEL
IMPOSSIBLE.
YOU GO TO CLASS AND YOU ARE
IMMEDIATELY TOLD TO GO SIT DOWN.
YOU CAN'T TALK.
YOU CAN'T MOVE.
I USED TO HAVE THIS PROBLEM.

MY ADVICE IS TO FIND SOMETHING YOU ARE
GOOD AT, AND FIGHT HARD TO EXCEL AT IT.

FIND YOUR STRENGTHS AND PURSUE THEM,
USING THEM TO WORK YOUR WAY AROUND
OTHER WEAKNESSES THAT YOU MAY HAVE.

32

I don't consider myself disabled in any way.

My learning difference has never gotten in the way of goals I have wanted to accomplish. I have continued to push myself through all my hardships and I have strived for excellence in academics, high moral standards and ideals. As I have worked to better my skills in the language, I have found that my true gift is in math and science.

I believe that each individual does have strengths and weaknesses and as long as you recognize each, you can flourish in life AND have fun learning.

Even though we may learn differently, we still can accomplish greatness in life. It takes perseverance and passion to overcome difficulty in learning but it can be done!

MY DYSGRAPHIA REMAINS A SERIOUS CHALLENGE.

SOME OF MY FRIENDS SAY I AM LUCKY TO BE ABLE TO USE A COMPUTER IN CLASS, BUT IF I COULD EXCHANGE A COMPUTER FOR THE ABILITY TO WRITE LEGIBLY,

I WOULD JUMP ON THAT DEAL.

I STARTED SITTING IN ON MY IEP IN SIXTH GRADE AND I BEGAN TO UNDERSTAND IT (LD) BETTER.

33

If I were given the opportunity to speak to a student who had just been diagnosed with a learning difference, I would want to share numerous thoughts regarding how to handle that information so he or she could proceed with a positive attitude. First, I would tell that person to understand his or her diagnosis and how it impacts learning. After considering one's specific learning difference, it is important to familiarize yourself with your learning style and learn the best way to study according to that style. Once you being studying according to your learning style (auditory, visual, kinesthetic, or some combination of the three), then make sure you receive appropriate accommodations according to your testing results. Next, make sure your school will support and embrace your learning difference and provide you with those accommodations. Some accommodations must be utilized during high school, or it is difficult to access those same accommodations while take the SAT, the ACT, or during college. I would also encourage someone just discovering his or her learning difference to locate a tutor who specializes in teaching students who learn differently. This person can provide tremendous support on assignments and teach you organizational and time management skills. These tend to be areas in which many students struggle; those while learning differences are apt to need extra support with them. When choosing a tutor, it is essential that rapport is easily established. Typically, a student spends at least an hour each week with his or her tutor. This is why it is crucial that you feel comfortable and can communicate easily with that person. Finally, the most important piece of advice I would give a student just discovering a learning difference is that this is not the end of the world. Be comfortable with who you are and be willing to discuss how you learn with others. I believe I have been successful during high school because I was encouraged by my mother and my learning specialist to strive for success and embrace who I am as a learner.

34

I like to think that, in my 18 years of life I have eaten enough chocolate to feed an entire forest's worth of chipmunks for a year. I also like to think that I have learned something about life, and about Learning Disabilities (LD). LD ends with the word disability which isn't really accurate. While it is different for everyone and there ARE tough parts about it, I wear my LD as a badge of pride

Be kind to the people around you. Those of us who are "broken" will be broken if we try to force our way alone, but we find friends, the people just like us, and we help each other. When one of us is bullied, we all stand up. When one of us needs help, we all pitch in. That's how we make it, not by picking at other people's weaknesses, but helping them with those flaws, knowing they'll do the same for us.

It's not all butterflies and rainbows though. There's a dark side to everything and it will be different for everyone. For me, it's often hard to control what comes out of my mouth. I'm lucky, because I'm a fairly nice person who doesn't insult people often but I also know that I can blurt out things that make other people uncomfortable or hurt their feelings.

Once you figure out what your struggle is, you can start to turn it to your advantage. I've learned how to control mine a little, but I've also learned how to use it to make people laugh, and I've learned it makes me honest, and it helps me be honest with myself.

The term "LD" is a label made by people who don't have it and was decided on when we knew next to nothing about LD. Now that we've done the research, we know that LDs have upsides. Each person's LD is different. For me, my mind goes off in all directions at once. One of my friends focuses on one thing for 20 minutes, and then goes to the next thing. To really be able to use your LD to your advantage, you have to figure out how it affects you. Once you do, use it. Don't try to suppress the abilities that make your "LD" and instead make them work for you instead of against you. I can tie everything in my papers together because I can see how they are connected. Some of my friends have talked their teachers into letting them take tests 20 minutes at a time; others have talked them into letting them take tests in a closet so there are no distractions. Make a strategy that will let you use your talents, then get people to let you use that strategy. LD is just a label made by people who don't have it; you have to play it to your strengths.

The last thing is to look down deep inside yourself, and find out who you are, and decide who you want to be.

If you look deep into yourself and think about all of who you are, even the parts that you hate, and how you can do better, you can learn to control your LD and use it to your advantage. At the end of the day, no one in the whole world can change you, if you know who you are then you can decide who you will be.

35

My advice to the young child would be this:

For starters, do not feel that you are all alone. You are not! Not only are there people who love you, there are many others that want to help you. You are a very special individual.

Make sure to pay attention in school. Take advantage of any special programs that you can help you out. Teachers are going to want to help you. Let them! Don't be afraid to ask for help. Asking for help is a good thing. Now, you may have to work harder than others, but that is okay, and will pay off in the end.

Please do not feel like you are different. Every single person is different. We are all unique. There is no need to feel ashamed. Hold your head high for who you are.

I would also suggest that you get involved with your school and your classmates. Whether you're into sports, or have an interest in music, or science or math, there is a team, or club for many diverse activities. Maybe you might want to run for student council, that's great too. You'll be involved, and having fun with others that have the same interest. Have some fun!

Lastly, please know that I speak from experience. I know what it is like. I've had to overcome learning issues in my life. I am graduating high school, and moving on to college. I have gotten involved in sports. I will be pitching for my high school as well as pitching in college.

You have your whole life in front of you. Work hard, and have fun.

36

I would tell a newly diagnosed student to be strong, have a lot of support, a sense of adventure and don't take life to seriously.

I think a student with a learning difference needs to be strong because the world likes to classify us into boxes. You are unique and will never fit into a contrived box.

You need to be strong because people aren't always kind when they find out you think in a different way than the "normal" students do. The adventure is trying to think outside the box on how to solve problems, how you need to work and get your schoolwork completed. You need to use technology, but also think old school in ways to stay organized, on task and on time.

You will need to find a way to keep calm and in your zen, such as music, exercise or meditating. You will run into a lot of unfair situations or people who are just plain nasty. You will run into this whether you have a learning difference or not. Learning to deal with this will take you far in life. Being able to ride the roller coaster of life will help you more than just at school. Enjoying the high side of the roller coaster is when you take in the kudos, which you save up for when you are on the downside of the coaster and you think no one understands what you are going through.

37

As someone who has struggled with learning differences my entire life, the best piece of advice I can offer a newly diagnosed student is to find what you are great at and passionate about and focus on that, not your disability. Every child has a gift. Do not allow yourself to be defined by your learning differences.

Clearly, I was not destined to be a great student. I was not a strong athlete or a winning debater. It wasn't until my middle school years that I discovered my gift; my voice and musical ear. Through music and musical theatre, I was able to build a confidence in myself that I simply could not achieve in an academic setting. For once, I was at the top of my class at something quite unique and incredible. School wasn't just something I had to get through. It was something I enjoyed and felt successful at as long as part of my day involved music.

You owe it to yourself to find whatever it is you are great at, and indulge in it. Surround yourself with likeminded people and don't, whatever you do, covet your disability. You are going to need their help and support to reach your full potential.

Looking back on it, I realize now that I always had strong mentors encouraging me at every stage of my life. In elementary school, it was a Speech Teacher who took me under her wing and taught me how to relate to peers when I was most anxious and depressed. She reassured me I would be o.k. if I just committed to getting through the hard times. She was right.

In middle school, it was my drama teacher who cast me as the lead role when everyone thought she was crazy; after all, I couldn't even read.

She was determined to prove her critics wrong and supported me in that role more than anyone could have imagined. I nailed that role!

Remember, just on the other side of every struggle, every challenge thrown your way, is the thrill of accomplishment. The most important thing is to never give up on yourself and your dreams.

Your disability will not define who you are or what you become. Your goal needs to be to find your hidden talents and then carve out your own path and journey to fulfill your life's plan.

38

When I was diagnosed with a learning disability my mother asked me if I thought it was fair if two people had to dig a hole and one had a shovel and the other had a spoon. I said that it was not fair. She said you are the person with the spoon.

It takes time but you will learn to understand what your difficulties are. Do not be afraid to ask for help or to be sure you understand a concept. If you are weak in some area you are probably strong in another area. Try to rely on your strength while working on the difficult areas. Many people have learning issues and no one can tell who they are. Be yourself.

39

A learning disability or difference can make you or break you. It is up to he or she to overcome an obstacle that can affect them greatly. One who has goals and strives for them will overcome anything. To reach goals, one must not expect things being handed to them. One should have the mindset that hard work does pay off.

One who receives a diagnosis of a learning disability should not let it be a barrier but a challenge. He or she can prove themselves that they can do anything. A newly diagnosed student with a learning difference should take on their disability and overcome it. The student should first understand their learning disability and figure out how they can improve themselves. Also, one should set high goals and gradually they will see a difference on their improvement.

A newly diagnosed student with a learning difference should understand they can ask for help when they are lost. If one finds their learning disability difficult, ask questions. One who handles everything by themselves will put a lot stress on their shoulders. With the help of loved ones and teachers, they are there for one who is lost. Also, one who does not put effort or care will not unfortunately overcome their learning disability.

Confidence is key to achieve one's goals. If one believes in themselves they can overcome all obstacles. Having a positive mind set can help boost confidence and overall well-being. Also, being confident affects one's work. All of one's positivity and confidence can help reach high goals. Hard work does pay off, believe in one's self and it will show.

Learning disability is not a barrier it is a challenge that will either make you or break you. If one puts their mind to it, one can overcome and achieve anything. With confidence and help from others one will be directed in the right path. Setting high goals will give one hopes and dreams to achieve. Also, it is up to he or she to overcome an obstacle that can affect one greatly.

40

I know that it is a scary time; teachers and parents all expect super kids. I see a lot of positive opportunities to address the learning disability. I would tell your parents and teachers, that a learning disability does not mean you can't learn. I would demonstrate this by going to turn off the lights, ask for a cell phone to be turned off. I would then tell them these things would not be possible without a person who had a learning disability. Thomas Edison invented the light bulb and Alexander Graham Bell invented the phone. The most important issue is focusing on solutions. That means little league baseball; by tracking the ball, the same way to track the pages. Karate or movement helps to integrate all your strengths.

Ask for help from all your teachers, family and friends. Keep a smile and focus on the positive. Enjoy your computer, now it is one of your tools for success.

41

Twice this year I have been asked to talk with junior high boys about not being ashamed about their learning disabilities. I shared with them that life is full of choices and those choices determine where you are going and how you are going to get there. When it comes to learning disabilities, a student can make one of the most important decisions of their school career. Either you can try hard and buckle down or you can take the easy way and do just what you need to do to get by.

When I was in junior high, I watched the older students do just enough to barely pass and they were satisfied with their work. They learned how to work the system and their grades showed it. Watching them, I realized that I wanted more. I knew there would be a lot of heartache along the way and it wasn't going to be easy.

During that time, my mom was also diagnosed with breast cancer and she taught me to not give up. She said that there were going to be challenges in our life and we can learn a lot from them. I took what she taught me and applied it to my schoolwork.

Now that my senior year comes to a close, I've shared with junior high students three strategies I have learned about learning disabilities. First, your teachers want to work with you to be successful. There are times that you might believe they are singling you out when in fact they are making sure you understand and have learned the material. Secondly, it may take you longer to study or complete assignments but it is worth it when you get to apply what you have learned to hands-on work.

I can remember not too long ago having the same opinion about why I needed to learn all this information, but my perspective has changed now. And finally, I told each student that he will be more proud of himself if he would set high goals and not give up.

I know I am fortunate enough to have parents that encouraged me to strive to do my very best. They supported me and provided tutors when I needed them. With their help along with my teachers, I am so proud of my own accomplishments. I explained to those students that this feeling of satisfaction in the last 18 months is incredible and I know they can set their goals high and reach them too.

For me, I know I made the right choice and I hope the boys I spoke with will continue to make the right choice too.

I believe that each of us is a role model and our choices influence what kinds of role model we choose to be.

As for me, I know I am a better person for making the choice I made.

42

Everyone has a gift to give, a talent to share, and a way to be. You need to find what's special about yourself and use it. A lot of who we are is because we were born that way. That's a good thing AND a bad thing. It's easy to see the physical things you were born with but not so much the inside things. I think the most important part is what we do with that information once we figure out exactly what it is. But sometimes that is very hard to do. So you need to be patient and be flexible because sometimes you don't know what you don't know. It's easier for others to "classify" or "profile" or "label".

You need to have courage to be you and get past someone elses idea of what you should be. Everyone decides what type of person they are going to be.

There will always be people that will try and stand in your way. Have the faith in yourself to KNOW you can learn, read and understand just like everyone else. You just might have to take a different path but that it might be a better path. You can dream and achieve and go on and do great things if you are willing to work hard and EARN it. You might feel that it isn't fair but who says life is fair? So don't feel like it's wrong to get help when you need to. Just don't waste opportunities that present themselves.

43

It is important to know that having a disability of any kind does not give anyone the permission to bully them. It has been my experience that after learning about my disability some of the other children in my school would harass and tease me because of it. Sometimes it was hard to even go to school because they made me feel so uncomfortable. Looking back, I realize that I was actually stronger than all of them; they were the ones with the true disability.

Embrace your disability! You are unique and special and this just enhances who you are. Never be ashamed of who or what you are, you have the ability to become whatever you desire.

Do not ever refuse to use the support systems that the schools have setup; if you do, this will just hinder your scholastic abilities and stress you out. These support systems are extremely helpful and have been very useful to me as I progressed through school.

Scot Hamilton said it best with his statement "The only disability in life is a bad attitude." When you're struggling with a negative aspect of your disability, take a deep breath and center on that motto. You can achieve so much more with an open and optimistic attitude than if you look around and only see what you cannot do.

44

Albert Einstein once said "Great spirits have always encountered violent opposition from mediocre minds." And it's true that those with different ideas, different views, and different strengths have always had to live lives filled with fear that the things that make them different will attract the attention of people who will never understand them.

I know what people think when they see me. They think that there is nothing wrong. They're right; there is nothing wrong. I just see the world a little differently from everyone else.

There was a time when I was laughed at for the way I thought. I was terrified of what other people would say if I told them that I was struggling with school, with making friends, and with just expressing myself to the people around me. I didn't know why I was never good at math or reading, so I shut everyone out. I never wanted anyone to know how much pain I was in, or how alone I felt. I remember awaking every morning as if that day would be the day that everything would fall apart. I became a walking time bomb. Would I be humiliated in front of everyone from my reading? Or would it be talking in front of class? Or maybe being laughed at by my own family?

Something that makes me even more beautiful is that I have the gift to choose and make my own decisions in life.

45

Growing up with a disability is never simple. From learning how to cope on a daily basis, to learning how to deal with strangers, and most importantly learning how to not let it control or define you. I'll admit, my disability doesn't affect me 100% of the time. I can go for days without anyone wondering if I have a problem. I can go through day to day society and survive on my own. But there was a time when I couldn't do that. A time where I thought it to be a fairytale to be able to have a single day where I'm currently standing. But I have fought day to night for the chance for that fairytale to come true. Battling throughout the day with the road blocks that were placed before me: an endless bitter battle.

The most powerful thing in the battle is to never doubt that you can defeat it. Don't ever put yourself down in not having the belief and the courage in defeating it. You can break free of the chains that were unknowingly cuffed on your wrists. You can break free of the invisible prison.

You have to become the cowardly lion. Find the courage, find the key. You will never be able to go throughout life without taking a leap forward without courage on your back.

Don't you ever take words for granted. If someone says you can't, it means you can though it may be more difficult than you can ever imagine. But with your strength combined with your courage you can redefine the words. You can twist the meaning so they become your strength so they work to your favor.

Keep those that you love and trust close to you, both mentally and physically. Without the support of those whom you love, the battle will be even more bitter. With the ones that you love, you have given yourself a goal to try to surprise them with overcoming the road blocks. And you have to grasp that goal and never let it go, lock it up and keep it prisoner. Throw it in a box, lock it up, and throw away the key.

46

The advice that I would give a student newly diagnosed with a learning difference would be to never give up and don't let anyone ever tell you that you can't do something or that you are not smart. I was diagnosed when I was very young, so I don't ever remember actually being told that I had a learning disability. It's just always been part of who I am. When I was younger, it was difficult and embarrassing for me. I hated being different than everyone else in my class. I would ask myself why do I have to have this and my classmates don't. My friends would ask me where I went when I would get pulled from our classroom. They would also ask why I had special classes. I would always tell them that I don't know and that it was because my parents made me.

When I was in 4th grade I had an incident with a classmate who was also on my football team. He was someone that I thought was my friend until one day he called me a SPED. I was devastated. My teacher was so upset about it, the next day she put on a presentation about famous people who all have learning differences. She explained to our class that we all learn differently and that we all have different talents. She handed out a sheet that had 50 famous people on it and pointed out that they all have some kind of learning difference. Having a learning difference did not stop them from being extremely successful people. Some of the famous names on the list were Magic Johnson, JFK, Cher, Tom Cruise and even Albert Einstein. The presentation made me feel much better about having a learning disability. My classmates learned that having a learning disability doesn't mean that you are not smart. Understanding the way you learn and learning strategies will help you be successful. So, my advice is to work hard, don't ever let a classmate get you down, take advantage of extra help and never give up on your dreams.

47

My Advice to Others....

Don't use your learning disability as an excuse for not getting your homework done. Use it as a reason for getting extra help!

Ask for assistance and get all of the extra help that you can get, even if it's every day. Don't be afraid or embarrassed to ask your teacher for extra help; you are the smart one. It is not a sign of weakness; it is a sign of strength!

Read a lot... Everything and anything! Use a computer for research and typing your homework; it will help a lot! It's sometimes hard at first and you might not like it, but you don't give up. You will eventually love it like I do!

Listen to everything that the teacher is saying but don't listen to anyone that tells you "you can't"; it should never become a part of your vocabulary. And, whatever you do, don't ever give up; just keep on going until you get to where it is that you want to be.

48

If I had to give advice to a child who is a newly diagnosed student with a learning difference, I would say that there are a lot of possibilities in life. One of the possibilities in life that I would encourage the child to go for is getting a quality education.

Getting a quality education is important for the child's educational development. Another possibility I would encourage the child to go for is learning social skills in order to communicate effectively while making friendships or forming relationships with others.

Another piece of advice that I would give a child who is a newly diagnosed with a learning difference is that there are ways to get support from someone if you are in need of help.

If you need support at school, you can always meet up with a guidance counselor to help you deal with school related issues. If you are in need of improving your grades in a specific class you can either get extra help from the teacher or get a tutor who is willing to do one-on-one instruction to help you succeed. Of course, you will always have your parents to guide you by teaching you life skills that will benefit you once you learn what it means to live independently.

49

Whether you want to be an Olympian, soldier, or president, even with a disability, you can achieve your dream. You only live one life and you need to take advantage of every opportunity and risk in order to achieve your goals.

You are not always going to like how hard you have to work. However, all that hard work will pay off and you will become a champion. To be successful, you will need to work. However, being successful with a learning disability is even harder. I do not want to beat around the bush; it is not easy. You will have to work twice as hard, if not harder, than most of your peers to become successful. You, on the other hand, will have resources and learning strategies to help you through it. You shouldn't rely completely on these resources, though. The resources are there to assist you with completing the work and not to help you get out of doing the work. Most people I have seen using support services struggle with the fact that they eventually have do tasks on their own.

Part of overcoming a disability is to become your own person and not rely on other people to do the work for you. If a person with disabilities figures this out right away, they are on the way to achieve their goals. Also, do not be afraid to ask questions. Teachers are more than willing to accommodate you if you meet them half way. By this I mean don't pretend that you understand something when you really don't. Many times when I asked questions, my peers also did not understand. I would ask questions a lot and sometimes I would ask the question more than once because I didn't understand it the first time.

My teachers at parent/teacher conferences always indicated that they appreciated my questions and were pleased that I asked. They always expressed that my willingness to ask questions would allow me to be successful in college. Also, a teacher will meet you half way if they recognize the amount of effort you are putting into your homework.

Another piece of advice is that you need to focus on what you need to do to be successful and not what your peers may say to you.

Some of your peers are going to be mean as they do not understand your learning disability. They are going to say that you get all the answers; you're not as smart as they are; and assume you don't work as hard as them because "you have got it easy." At first, this really bothered me because I did not like that people thought I was not as smart as they are or believed they are. It made me feel less important. You can't let that bother you, though. You have to push through that feeling. I knew that I needed the resources and learning strategies and I wanted to do well in school and pursue a college education. With this in mind, I stopped caring about what my peers though, and focused on what I needed to do to be successful and achieve good grades.

Not only did I learn learning strategies to overcome my learning disability but also life strategies. Through my working with the support services, I learned life strategies in planning, organizing, and prioritizing. All these skills are important as I enter college. Many teachers tell me that these skills will play a large part in my success in college. Therefore, I benefitted from learning these skills of which I would not have had the opportunity without needing to seek services.

At this point, I am ranked fifth in my class and prepared to go to college in the fall.

Everyone with a learning disability has the opportunity to obtain support services and learn strategies to overcome their learning disability. These recourses are there to assist you in being successful not only in school but also in life.

Again, not only did I learn how to work with learning disability, but also I learned skills to prepare me to be successful as I enter my next phase of education. You should embrace the opportunity to obtain these resources and not be ashamed. Just as I have done in high school, you also can be successful and achieve your dreams.

50

I was only 4 when first diagnosed with my specific learning disability. I vaguely remember my mom talking to my Aunt saying I was like a "new" child since I got the right help at school. I assume this was because I went from hating school to actually enjoying it. I remember thinking "I'm a new child?" It was funny. I guess that's why it stuck with me. My mom was encouraging my Aunt to have my cousins tested early because they were having issues at school. Unfortunately my Aunt waited, so my cousins were finally diagnosed in their mid teens.

It is sad. If a child is a prodigy at music or science and math, no one would deny that student access to an instrument or text book, but when it comes to learning to read or write, parents, because of fear and denial, refuse their children access to tools that can help. Had I been old enough, I would have given my cousins some of the advice I will share with you now. Stick with the program. I had to go to a different room for reading or writing and an Exceptional Student facilitator helped keep track of assignments. It was embarrassing and it seemed everyone was treating me like a baby.

After 12 years in the program, I read, write and do math at a college level, and I take honors level classes. Without the special attention, I may not have even considered college, much less completed high school.

Use technology to assist you. When I do service work, its typically to help record books on tape for other students with learning and visual disabilities. Because they helped me so much in middle school, I know personally how much audio books can help students keep up with reading and literature. Some other things that help me include a date planner to keep track of projects and assignments and using a computer compensates for bad handwriting.

Most recently, I started using a smart phone to combine almost all these activities using one tool. I text myself reminders about homework, I take photos of the teachers whiteboard notes, I record my rehearsals and make voice memos to review later. Cell phones are probably banned in your school. I have the same problem. In my opinion smart phones are beneficial to learning challenged students and using this technology in schools will need to be reassessed soon.

Do research about your diagnosis. Be sure to look at it's academic and emotional effects. My parents and teachers only talked about academic goals, such as "respond to writing prompt" or "turn in assignments". I started noticing I didn't understand jokes and I often didn't know how to react in certain situations. Privately, I cried a lot. I was heartbroken because I didn't seem to have any friends. It wasn't until I read my own diagnosis and what it meant socially that I accepted the differences as my normal. Now, I have good friends and perform in one of the best high school jazz bands in the country.

Sticking with the exceptional student program, using available assistive technology and doing research about specific learning disabilities have helped me become successful at life so far.

I plan to use these tools to continue into college and beyond.

51

My advice for you is to never give up. It may take longer for you to accomplish life challenges. However remember to be patient with yourself. One of the most important days of my life was when I went to Virginia's Department of Motor Vehicles to get my permit. I was looking forward to this day for a long time. It took me four attempts to get my permit because of my learning disability. This is my story and why you should never give up.

I used the computer station for the first three times I took the test. The first part of the test was to identify the road signs. On my first attempt, this was the easy part. I had studied this the most and had it down pat. Question by question I read every single word carefully. I reassured myself, 10 questions to go and I'm on number 9! I'm doing great.

The final question popped up on my screed: a *blank* yellow sign. The first two choices were obviously not the answer. My remaining choices were Caution or Warning signs. I was on my last question on the part of the test. I began to visualize the two signs. They were both yellow signs with the same shape. Okay, I picked the Caution Sign. The new screen popped up, "Incorrect answer Choice." I had failed the test. I felt a sense of disappointment but I wasn't devastated. I knew I could take the test again and learn from my mistake.

The second and third times I took the test I made it through the road signs. Both times I moved onto the second part of the test which is general knowledge. Before the tests, my mother quizzed me and I knew every answer, but during the tests, I could not relax, and my learning disability affected my reading comprehension. I failed the second section twice.

When I didn't pass my permit test the third time I was frustrated because I knew the material. Now I had to go back to retake my Driver's Education Course. When I didn't pass my third time, frustrating as it was, I knew I wouldn't give up. I made flash cards and used the two weeks I had to wait to restudy for the test. Instead of thinking I would never get my permit, I was determined and knew I could do it. I went back to the DMV and requested to have the test on paper. I told myself, this is just like a pop quiz. I can do this. I knew I could use my reading strategies. I underlined key words and circled important parts. This made it easier for me to read the test to myself and concentrate. I passed!

Even though it took a long journey to get my permit, I never lost my optimism or my persistence.

I am a motivated and hard working student. This is my story, and why I know I will be successful in life.

This is my advice for you. You are always going to have to work harder than others. You are always going to have to be more persistent. You are always going to have to ask questions when you are confused and you shouldn't feel embarrassed or let anyone make you feel stupid. You will always have a learning disability but you will find ways to cope with your struggles and succeed.

52

Having a learning disability in public school can be very challenging. As I reflect back on my school years I spent lot of time wondering why everything was so difficult..

Something that helped me was Howard Gardener's psychological theory about people and multiple intelligences. He believed that there are seven different categories that are a part of the multiple intelligence theory; verbal, logical, physical, visual, musical, intrapersonal, and interpersonal. Howard Gardner believed that all people have multiple forms of intelligences; these multiple intelligences can be strengthened and nurtured or weakened and ignored. I would tell them to identify what kind of smart they are so they could use their strengths to their advantage and improve their weaknesses.

That's what I did. I realized that I had to nurture my strengths of being a visual learner and use it to my advantage in school. I have found in public schools that most students are word smart and number-smart (or mathematically minded). It takes a special teacher to teach all kinds of students. I've been fortunate to have had some of those special teachers that seem to be able to differentiate for all kinds of learners. However, when you don't have one of those teachers, you have to learn to teach yourself, using your strengths. I have had to go home at night and re-teach myself the material and find resources that catered to my strengths. This can be challenging, and time consuming, but I would tell the child that it is worth it. Being able to teach myself has been a positive experience that has helped me through my high school years and I believe has prepared me for college.

It took me a long time to realize that learning to work hard is positive.

SELF-ADVOCACY HAS BEEN ONE OF MY
GREATEST STRENGTHS AND HAS HELPED ME
COUNTLESS TIMES BOTH THROUGH
SCHOOLING AND MY LIFE.

ON ONE HAND IT FURTHERS YOUR OWN SELF-
DISCOVERY,
UNDERSTANDING BETTER WHO YOU ARE AND
HOW YOU WORK.

ASPERGER'S SYNDROME

53

(My daughter) has been unforgettable kid since she was a toddler. She looked different than other kids in her school with pale blond hair, giant blue eyes and a body bigger than her peers. She often moved left when instructed to move right and at age 7 told her second grade teacher she needed 'a few minutes in the hall to gather my thoughts'. At 9 years old the diagnosis of Asperger Syndrome made all the sense in the world as we searched for reasons for her unique and may times confounding and quirky qualities. We danced to the beat of a different drummer in our family.

With a diagnosis of Aspergers – she could put a name on her feelings of separateness, but she knew that she still needed to work out her unique path in the world regardless of the label pinned on it.

She looked at life through an extraordinary lens and she was determined to honor the gift.

As teachers and many times we, her parents, tried to encourage her to conform and comply at school and home because we knew her life would be easier if she did, she rejected our advice. She set out to do it her way. She couldn't take the shortcuts in Math class and she couldn't obey her parents unless she understood the 'why'. The life of a child on the autism spectrum is often wracked with difficulty of perception and her life was and is no exception. Her support system was often a stiff and clumsy collaboration of people and steps. Neurologically typical peers eventually realized they couldn't easily connect with her... so they moved on to kids with who they could easily mesh. Teachers saw keen intellect and formed expectations, many times to have their expectations unfulfilled because of her literal thinking, organizational deficit and a processing delay combined with a stringent desire to 'do it her way'.

Many teachers made her feel as though she didn't live up to her potential. As her parents we were exhausted from the clumsy dance of ensuring that our intelligent child was challenged and her deficits supported at the same time. And truthfully, our sense of frustration at balancing what the world expected of her and what she delivered was often clear to her.

Despite intense frustration in her formative years, our daughter participated in a multitude of extracurricular activities. She eagerly attended social skills programs and braved sleep away summer camps designed for kids with special needs. She volunteered at animal shelters and in recent years developed great interest in acting and film making. She attended many programs designed to broaden her natural pattern of social interaction which was typically limiting and self oriented. It became clear to us that she needed to be fully included in her community. Real inclusion means being on the giving and receiving end of human interaction. Many kids with special needs tend to be on the receiving end as they try to improve deficits in their functioning. Through her social skills class at her school she logged in 35 hours of community service during her junior year in high school, working every Saturday on different community projects. She was beginning to understand that her role in helping others both gave service to her community and empowered her. Along these lines, the last two summers were spent at Farm and Wilderness camps in Vermont – a 'graduation' from special needs camp to "typical" camp where she was supported as all kids were but the camp was physically and emotionally challenging. Teens work on a local farm for 7 weeks each summer. On a mountainside, this farm focuses on creating community responsibility and personal responsibility among its farmers. This past summer she volunteered for the 'Service Corps' work project team which provided cleanup assistance to local community members and farms, all related to recovery efforts from the devastation in the area caused by Hurricane Irene.

Our daughter has struggled greatly with the camp rule of rising at dawn to do chores, and understanding and caring about how her actions impacted others (related to "theory of mind" which is often missing in individuals on the autism spectrum). When faced with the hard choice of being sent home or staying at camp and being part of her community in her actions and thinking – she found a way to advocate for herself with camp leaders; explaining her limitations and her desire to contribute to the community and the difficult projects at play, she offered a service for which she would be completely responsible for at a different time of day. She learned that in a 'work and team' environment, where she was different from her peers in many ways – it was her responsibility to explain to her team why she needed to sometimes accomplish things using a different route or method and ensure that her contribution was appropriate and fulfilled her obligation. She began to develop 'theory of mind'. She greatly enjoyed her work in the community and forged relationships with the local people she helped in her work on the service corps.

Also, over the last few years, She has been exposed to film making and acting in those amateur films – and she found a place that felt like home. She realized that as she took on a role to portray or discovered a short film idea to turn into digital art, she was fully alive. She has now acted in several short films and uses her newly found skill of understanding that other's perspectives may be different and equally important as hers, to enhance her craft of acting and film making. She knows now that the message she portrays will be interpreted by others and in order to succeed she must put herself in the audience's mindset, an extraordinary accomplishment in thinking and perspective for an individual on the autism spectrum.

Now in her senior year of high school she no longer needs regular parental involvement in her school business. If she needs an accommodation she usually advocates for herself. She is still keenly aware of her social differences but has found a place with her peers that is respectful and relatively easy.

She is comfortable talking to others about what it's like to have Aspergers and how she feels about society's views. She is quick to clarify 'the ins and outs of life with Aspergers' for others who show interest.

Our daughter was recently accepted to a University on the East Coast, where she will attend as a freshman Film Major in the fall. Many days of late she can be found at play rehearsal where, when she is waiting for her next set of lines or song, can be found dancing backstage… not the clumsy dance of her earlier life… but a graceful dance of joy at having found her place. She still struggles often with circumstances that offend her sensibilities or overwhelm her preference for sameness yet she has developed the tools to cope with her frustration and draws on those tools often. She is brave and willing to put her toe into the dance of 'normal' in hopes that each time she times, learning the steps will be a little easier and her feeling of belonging and personal fulfillment will make her heart sing again and again.

54

Having Asperger's Syndrome is not a death sentence, merely a blessing in disguise. Yes, you are different and will continue to be different, but really what this means is you get to see the world through unadulterated eyes. You will learn to appreciate people not only for their gifts, but also their weaknesses, because while they may be irksome, they are part of the identity of a person. In other words, they help to make a person unique and on that regard they are priceless.

If you are like me, you will struggle in social situations and as a result you will, in all likelihood, have less friends. Do not fret, though because as the old aphorism says "quality, not quantity." In other words, the friendships you do form will have a unique value and strength. The friends who can see past the faults and imperfections in you and still value you are lifelong friends. In short, you may not be the best at making friends, but you will certainly understand both the nature and concept of friendship better than most.

You may experience toils and errors in self-expression, and you might even anger some people unintentionally. Do not worry though, because you probably will mean well and intentions never stay masked by actions for too long. This is a quality you might even be valued for later in life, as honest is increasingly rare, and while the blunt truth is sometimes hurtful, when it does slip out it forces people to rethink their ways. Again, while it might not always be evident, you will have a greater understanding of empathy than most. Do not disregard the opinions of others, though it might be an implicit comment on the varieties of ignorance. Lastly, you will have a unique perseverance that will shine in your post educational years. So while your intelligence did not always manifest itself within the confines of school, it will in the occupational world. Above all, remember that you are not an alien, or weird, you are simply a different kind of normal.

55

It is OK to be different and unique. Having a learning difference means that you learn things in a different way than other kids. That doesn't make you weird... a learning different doesn't define who you are or what you can do in your life. I would tell the child that he/she is unique and that it is Awesome to be Unique!

It is very scary having to try new things and to "test" what works or what doesn't. It is okay to be scared, but don't let that fear stop you from trying. There are times in every person's life when they get scared, it doesn't matter if you have a learning difference or not.

With my learning difference, I wanted to stay in "my box" where everything was comfortable for me. My parents always pushed me to try new things like pee-wee football and piano lessons, and band. At first, I didn't want to try them, but looking back, trying these things helped me grow and learn more about myself. I didn't succeed at everything I tried, but that is okay. I was able to make friends and become more social and get "out of my comfort zone".

Growing up, many people (teachers, doctors, family friends) always talked about what I couldn't do or achieve. That was very frustrating for both me and my parents. I am proof that any person with a learning difference can achieve their goals, whatever they may be. I have been active in my high school, have some awesome friends, have applied and been accepted into 3 colleges, and have a wonderful support system! It hasn't been easy for me, but I have made it this far! I want to be able to work with animals and be a living example to others that persons with learning differences can make a difference in the world we live in! No matter what situation we are given or faced with, each person can make a difference in the world and achieve their goals! Never give up! "Shoot for the moon. Even if you miss, you'll land among the stars." Brian Littrel Quote.

56

First off, do not panic if you have been diagnosed with Asperger Syndrome. It isn't the end of the world. In fact, it may be a new, better start for you. You haven't changed. You've simply gained some insight into why you think differently from others, and I want to make it clear that that *is* the case. I'll put it simply. Absolutely *nothing* is wrong with you. The word "syndrome" means "illness," but you aren't sick.

You can learn, and you can learn just as well as anybody else. You just learn in a different way than they do. The truth is that you do not have a learning "disability," but a learning difference.

Now that that's out of the way, I want you to know that your recent diagnosis isn't a bad thing. On the contrary, you're lucky that they diagnosed you now instead of later. It means that people can help you find the accommodations that you need to learn in the way that works best for you, and they can give you those accommodations. If you hadn't been diagnosed with your learning difference, you might be struggling in school, and nobody would know why.

Many people who we think of as geniuses today were considered strange, or even crazy, at some point in their lives. Some of them were seen this way due to unrecognized learning differences (some scientists believe that Albert Einstein may have been autistic), but now we admire those same people, and some of the ones who are still alive today are rich and famous. With time and the right accommodations, you yourself could prove to be one of the greatest minds in history.

57

Dear Stranger,

I'm not going to pretend I can conceive of how strange and unsettling feelings you have over your diagnosis. Although I remember my discovery well, I cannot even fathom the mix of hurt and relief you must feel. I remember the wash of realization I had when it all made sense; I assume you do as well. I am hoping you use this information as I have; not as a crutch, but as an inspiration to move further and push harder, now knowing the severe disadvantage you have. View this anomaly not as a curse, but as a gift; you have what poets and artists search years for – motivation. The stage is set – you are now free of some confusion. Use this information carefully; people will inevitably treat you "differently"; but only if you allow them to do so. Use this clarity not as a weapon, but as a tool, and take whatever gifts someone gives you, always with the intention to give back in one way or another. If your school offers help and there's even a slight chance you may want to use it, do exactly that. You are your own worst enemy if you think you can do this alone. We have been burdened with a crutch, but blessed with a mind and a point of view eager to be released. You are not your IEP. We are not the bombastically-named disorders which chain us. I am not Autism – I am ME. You are you, and as cliché as it sounds, you must go out there and be the best you can be, because, well, why not?

A friend

58

Ever since childhood, I have had tremendous interest in the world around me. The physical world and real, tangible, and natural things have always attracted my interest. This attraction to the natural world has sparked a tremendous and growing interest in science and mathematics. My parents have always been supportive of my interests and have encouraged me to be myself, and to "shoot for the stars". I have always appreciated this encouragement and recognize the valuable contribution of the support to my well-being from my father and mother.

Although I have cultivated a love of learning and of classroom and study, it was not always that way. In my first three years of primary education, I was in private school setting with a curriculum that accentuated reading and writing, with very little science and mathematics. I struggled through these early grades and fell behind in my academic growth. In 2004 I was diagnosed with Asperger's syndrome, a minor trait in the autistic spectrum. At that time, it was recommended that I be placed in a different learning environment. The transition that followed, from private school to public school was pivotal in my academic career and life.

In public school, my grades improved dramatically. I was able to cope better with this environment, my teachers, and my peers. I started to become less socially awkward, and I was able to get others to understand me better. In sixth grade I began to pursue extra studies of science on my own to enhance my school work. I read an entire earth science book and felt quite knowledgeable about the subject. In seventh grade, I embarked on a period of two full years with a 4.0 grade point average! In seventh grade I began to study chemistry and physics, and my love of science became permanent. During the summer before my junior year in high school, I took a summer college introductory chemistry course that I found truly challenging, but inspirational. I subsequently pursued advanced placement studies in chemistry in the fall semester, a favorite course of mine that semester.

Characteristics of Asperger's syndrome are fixation on things, and the potential for over-analyzing problems. These characteristics of the syndrome have caused me significant issues in my early life, but I find that my awareness of these pitfalls has allowed me to develop good coping skills, and I am able to compensate and avoid the problems that typically follow. A major wakeup call and impetus for the further development of my coping mechanisms was my failure on a rigidly timed, advanced placement exam. It took me the entire summer of my senior year to put this failure into perspective and successfully reinstitute my motto to "never give up and never accept failure". I enrolled in pre-calculus at the local community college, and the enjoyment I experienced for this class has carried over to my advanced placement studies in calculus and physics.

I find that I learn in a different way than others, but I am fully capable of hard and challenging work. My interest in science and mathematics has led to my focus on engineering and my current plans to present a chemical or aerospace engineering research project this year. I intend to complete undergraduate and graduate work, and entertain the possibility of a doctoral in engineering. My dream is to more fully develop my understanding of the world and to make significant contribution to others in their understanding of the physical world.

ACKNOWLEDGEMENTS

The RiSE Scholarship Foundation, Inc.'s ability to grow as an organization and to bring awareness to students who learn differently would not have been possible without the insight, gracious support and encouragement of our loving family and friends. You know who you are!

Individually I need to thank Steve, T. and H. (my patient and loving family, who have allowed me to talk their ears off of how awesome each and every family is that RiSE is able to help).

I would like to thank our pediatrician, Dr. Joy Maxey. The care you have for your patients, the attention to detail and the extensive research you are continually interested in, not only inspired me but also has changed the course of our life!

Special thanks to the interns that have worked with and for RiSE, teaching and learning in equal measures: Kerry, Sophie, Alex, Julie, and Liz.

To the RiSE Scholarship Foundation, Inc. award applicants who continually encourage us with every interaction, we want to thank you for sharing and contributing to the bigger picture!

Made in the USA
Middletown, DE
19 December 2014